Understanding
American History

The Internment of Japanese Americans

David Robson

Bruno Leone
Series Consultant

ReferencePoint
Press®

San Diego, CA

© 2014 ReferencePoint Press, Inc.
Printed in the United States

For more information, contact:
ReferencePoint Press, Inc.
PO Box 27779
San Diego, CA 92198
www. ReferencePointPress.com

LIBRARY OF CONGRESS CATALOGING-IN-PUBLICATION DATA

Robson, David, 1966-
  The internment of Japanese Americans / by David Robson.
    pages cm. -- (Understanding American history)
  Includes bibliographical references and index.
  ISBN-13: 978-1-60152-592-5 (hardback)
  ISBN-10: 1-60152-592-3 (hardback)
  1. Japanese Americans--Evacuation and relocation, 1942-1945. 2. World War, 1939-1945--Concentration camps--United States. 3. World War, 1939-1945--Japanese Americans. I. Title.
  D769.8.A6R65 2014
  940.53'1773--dc23
                                                    2013017894

Contents

Foreword

America's Puritan ancestors—convinced that their adopted country was blessed by God and would eventually rise to worldwide prominence—proclaimed their new homeland the shining "city upon a hill." The nation that developed since those first hopeful words were uttered has clearly achieved prominence on the world stage and it has had many shining moments but its history is not without flaws. The history of the United States is a virtual patchwork of achievements and blemishes. For example, America was originally founded as a New World haven from the tyranny and persecution prevalent in many parts of the Old World. Yet the colonial and federal governments in America took little or no action against the use of slave labor by the southern states until the 1860s, when a civil war was fought to eliminate slavery and preserve the federal union.

In the decades before and after the Civil War, the United States underwent a period of massive territorial expansion; through a combination of purchase, annexation, and war, its east–west borders stretched from the Atlantic to the Pacific Oceans. During this time, the Industrial Revolution that began in eighteenth-century Europe found its way to America, where it was responsible for considerable growth of the national economy. The United States was now proudly able to take its place in the Western Hemisphere's community of nations as a worthy economic and technological partner. Yet America also chose to join the major western European powers in a race to acquire colonial empires in Africa, Asia, and the islands of the Caribbean and South Pacific. In this scramble for empire, foreign territories were often peacefully annexed but military force was readily used when needed, as in the Philippines during the Spanish-American War of 1898.

Toward the end of the nineteenth century and concurrent with America's ambitions to acquire colonies, its vast frontier and expanding industrial base provided both land and jobs for a new and ever-growing wave of immigrants from southern and eastern Europe. Although America had always encouraged immigration, these newcomers—Italians, Greeks, and eastern European Jews, among others—were seen as different from the vast majority of earlier immigrants, most of whom were from northern and western Europe. The presence of these newcomers was treated as a matter of growing concern, which in time evolved into intense opposition. Congress boldly and with calculated prejudice set out to create a barrier to curtail the influx of unwanted nationalities and ethnic groups to America's shores. The outcome was the National Origins Act, passed in 1924. That law severely reduced immigration to the United States from southern and eastern Europe. Ironically, while this was happening, the Statue of Liberty stood in New York Harbor as a visible and symbolic beacon lighting the way for people of *all* nationalities and ethnicities seeking sanctuary in America.

Unquestionably, the history of the United States has not always mirrored that radiant beacon touted by the early settlers. As often happens, reality and dreams tend to move in divergent directions. However, the story of America also reveals a people who have frequently extended a helping hand to a weary world and who have displayed a ready willingness—supported by a flexible federal constitution—to take deliberate and effective steps to correct injustices, past and present. America's private and public philanthropy directed toward other countries during times of natural disasters (such as the contributions of financial and human resources to assist Haiti following the January 2010 earthquake) and the legal right to adopt amendments to the US Constitution (including the Thirteenth Amendment freeing the slaves and the Nineteenth Amendment granting women the right to vote) are examples of the nation's generosity and willingness to acknowledge and reverse wrongs.

With objectivity and candor, the titles selected for the Understanding American History series portray the many sides of America, depicting both its shining moments and its darker hours. The series strives to help readers achieve a wider understanding and appreciation of the American experience and to encourage further investigation into America's evolving character and founding principles.

Important Events in the History of Japanese Internment

1922
In *Ozawa v. United States*, the Supreme Court reaffirms that Asian immigrants are not eligible for naturalization.

1920
California Alien Land Law prohibits leasing land to "aliens ineligible to citizenship." By 1925 at least twelve more western and midwestern states pass a similar law.

1941
On December 7 Japan attacks the US military base at Pearl Harbor; the United States declares war on Japan the next day; within the week, the FBI detains 1,370 Japanese Americans it classifies as "dangerous enemy aliens."

1944
In March forty-three Japanese American soldiers are arrested for refusing to participate in combat training at Fort McClellan, Alabama, as a protest against treatment of their families in US camps; in June Jerome becomes the first camp to close when the last inmates are transferred to Rohwer, Arkansas; in October the 442nd Regimental Combat Team rescues an American battalion that has been cut off and surrounded by the enemy.

1900 / 1941 1942 1943 1944

1913
California Alien Land Law prohibits "aliens ineligible to citizenship," meaning all Asian immigrants, from owning land or property.

1935
A small number of first generation Japanese immigrants, known as Issei, begin the process of obtaining citizenship under a congressional act making them eligible for citizenship if they have served honorably in the US armed forces and are permanent residents of the United States.

1943
In February the 442nd Regimental Combat Team, made up entirely of Japanese Americans, is activated; in June the US Supreme Court upholds the constitutionality of the curfew and exclusion orders; in September, after filling out a long questionnaire, internees deemed loyal to the United States begin to leave Tule Lake for other camps, while so-called disloyal internees arrive from other camps to Tule Lake.

1942
In February President Franklin D. Roosevelt signs Executive Order 9066, which sets the stage for the forced removal and incarceration of Japanese Americans; a few weeks later General John DeWitt issues Public Proclamation No. 1, which creates military areas in Washington, Oregon, California, and parts of Arizona and declares the federal government's right to remove German, Italian, and Japanese aliens and anyone of Japanese ancestry away from the nation's West Coast, if necessary; in August and September the first internees begin arriving at internment camps in Idaho, Colorado, Utah, and Arkansas.

1945
Restrictions preventing Japanese American resettlement on the West Coast are removed in January; in May the surrender of Germany ends the war in Europe; three months later the United States drops the atomic bomb on the Japanese cities of Hiroshima and Nagasaki, and Japan surrenders on August 14.

1988
H.R. 442 is signed into law by President Ronald Reagan, providing individual payments of $20,000 to each surviving internee and a $1.25 billion education fund.

1948
Truman signs the Japanese American Evacuation Claims Act in July, a measure to compensate Japanese Americans for certain economic losses attributable to their forced evacuation.

1981
The Commission on Wartime Relocation and Internment of Civilians (CWRIC) holds a public hearing in Washington, DC, as part of its investigation into the internment of Japanese Americans during World War II.

1945   **1955**   **1965**   **1975**   **1985**

1970
A resolution is announced by the Japanese American Citizens League's Northern California–Western Nevada District Council calling for reparations for the World War II incarceration of Japanese Americans.

1990
The first nine redress payments are made at a Washington, DC, ceremony, with 107-year-old Reverend Mamoru Eto of Los Angeles receiving the first check.

1979
Representative Mike Lowry introduces the World War II Japanese-American Human Rights Violations Act into Congress, which proposes direct payments of $15,000 per internee.

1946
Tule Lake in California closes in March, although many of those evacuated are elderly, impoverished, or mentally ill and have no place to go; in the summer the 442nd Regimental Combat Team is given a heroes' welcome at the White House by President Harry S. Truman.

1983
The CWRIC issues its formal recommendations to Congress concerning redress for Japanese Americans interned during World War II, including the call for individual payments of $20,000 to each of those who spent time in the internment camps and are still alive.

7

The Defining Characteristics of Japanese Internment

In 1782 French American writer J. Hector St. John de Crèvecoeur coined the term *melting pot* to describe his newly adopted country, the United States. In his work *Letters from an American Farmer*, de Crèvecoeur ponders what it means to be an American. For decades, immigrants from England, Sweden, Scotland, France, Germany, Ireland, and Netherlands had swarmed the shores of colonial America in search of religious freedom and opportunity; one's place of birth became less important than forging a future in which people from all backgrounds lived and worked side by side in this newly independent land. De Crèvecoeur captures this spirit in his popular collection of missives, and in his most famous letter he writes, "Here individuals of all nations are melted into a new race of men, whose labor and posterity will one day cause great changes in the world."[1]

De Crèvecoeur's words defined an American ideal in which differences between people fell away to engender one people, united by a common purpose. Yet in the more than 230 years since, American history has revealed a more complex truth, as religious and ethnic divisions have sometimes led to fear, prejudice, and discrimination. Although the United States began its life as a nation of immigrants, newcomers have often been eyed suspiciously by those already settled. Many feared an influx of strangers who looked and acted differently from them, thinking these newcomers might take their jobs and change their way of life. In the late nineteenth and early twentieth centuries immigrants from East Asia—China, Japan, and Korea—entered the United States. Their presence frightened many people and in time led to one of the most unjust events in American history.

Attack and Internment

On the morning of December 7, 1941, the nation of Japan attacked the American naval base at Pearl Harbor in Hawaii. Thousands of American servicemen were killed. The next day American president Franklin

The Mochida family waits for the bus that will take them to an internment camp, a scene shot by famed photographer Dorothea Lange in May 1942 in Hayward, California. Identification tags helped keep the family members together after they were forced to leave their home and nursery business in the San Francisco Bay Area.

D. Roosevelt announced that war had been declared on Japan, thereby ushering in US involvement in World War II. In the hours after the attack on Pearl Harbor, FBI agents arrested scores of Japanese men who were non–US citizens living in the United States. Twelve hundred men in all were taken from their homes and detained without being charged with a crime. Authorities were seeking anyone with any ties to the Japanese Empire. In the weeks and months that followed, more than 110,000 men, women, and children—most of them American citizens—were ordered from their homes and sent to internment camps far from home.

There, Japanese American families were subjected to stark and often humiliating conditions. Armed guards patrolled the camps; long lines for food, water, and showers were common. Those incarcerated had little space and even less privacy in the makeshift barracks in which they lived. Rights guaranteed by the US Constitution were disregarded; freedom of movement was suspended. Families got along however they could, with no knowledge of when they might be set free. Some internees seethed with rage at the harsh treatment by their country of birth and pledged loyalty to Japan, their ancestral home. Others remained loyal to an American government that did not remain loyal to them.

Release and Renewal

When the war ended in 1945 Japanese Americans had to piece their lives back together and try to move on. During the years that followed, most Americans tried to forget the misguided and racist act of their government, but those interned and their children could not forget. They lobbied the US government, seeking some sort of apology, an acknowledgement of wrongdoing, but they received only silence. Not until the late 1980s did the federal government acknowledge what had been done to so many Americans and try to make amends.

The account of Japanese American internment camps is composed of many stories—stories of mothers and fathers, sons and daughters. During their more than three years of imprisonment, internees found joy as well as sorrow, forgiveness as well as anger. Their unique and heartrending journey from darkness to light remains relevant today, especially because of recent threats to the United States. Since at least the 1990s, international terrorists groups have worked to attack democratic nations around the world and kill their citizens. In the aftermath of the September 11, 2001, attacks on New York City and Washington, DC, carried out by a group of extremists of the Muslim faith, some American voices called for detaining and imprisoning followers of Islam. Such calls echoed an earlier time when Americans suspected that all people of Japanese ancestry were potential spies or saboteurs. The lessons of the Japanese American internment camps of the 1940s are still being learned in the twenty-first century.

Chapter 1

What Conditions Led to Internment of Japanese Americans?

From its earliest years, the United States welcomed people from all over the world to its shores. Yet that welcome was also tempered by a deep suspicion of newcomers and at times led to discrimination, violence, and detention. European immigration to the United States spiked between 1899 and 1910. Italians and Slavs, Irish and Polish people made the often difficult journey across the Atlantic Ocean and into New York Harbor, where they were greeted by the Statue of Liberty and her glowing torch, symbols of freedom. They came to find better jobs, greater financial opportunity, and the chance to live as they chose. While they were often seen as interlopers by those already living in America, the immigrants themselves typically found some measure of comfort and solace by living in close proximity to people from their own ethnic or religious groups. Thus, Jews lived in neighborhoods with other Jews; Italians congregated in sections where their fellow countrymen already owned homes or rented apartments. Regardless of their backgrounds, immigrants to the United States worked not only to make a living but to acclimate themselves to their new country and way of life.

First Wave

East Asian immigrants began streaming into the United States as early as the 1850s and were just as unwelcome, if not more so, than their European counterparts because they looked so different from those of Western ancestry. Between 1851 and 1882 only about three hundred thousand Chinese refugees landed on American shores; a majority settled their families on the West Coast—California, Oregon, and Washington. Chinese men found low-paying but steady jobs in mines and on railroad construction sites, but their presence led to resentment among white Americans, many of whom complained that these new immigrants were taking their jobs. Consequently, discriminatory state laws were passed regarding Chinese miners, and business licenses were often denied to these struggling immigrants.

This racially motivated discrimination became part of the wider American culture. Newspapers portrayed Asian people—and the Chinese in particular—as inferior and deserving of ill treatment. "[The common phrase] 'Not a Chinaman's chance' perfectly captured the plight of Chinese immigrants in the 19th century and a good part of the 20th century," says scholar Guofang Li, "because the Chinese immigrant had none of the constitutional rights extended to all persons in the United States."[2]

This denial of basic rights helped slow Chinese immigration to a trickle, as did the Chinese Exclusion Act of 1882. Passed by the US Congress, this new law suspended the immigration of Chinese workers into the country for a period of ten years. "And during such suspension," the law read, "it shall not be lawful for any Chinese laborer to come, or, having so come after the expiration of said ninety days, to remain within the United States."[3]

But while Chinese immigrants bore the brunt of the congressional act, other East Asians made new inroads into the American system. Beginning in about 1891, immigrants from Japan began streaming into the United States seeking opportunities that their own country could not provide. Over the course of fifteen years, more than two hundred thousand Japanese entered the United States. Before long, their presence would change the course of American history.

The Issei Arrive

Although many Americans were happy to see Chinese immigration at a standstill, the nation still needed cheap labor. The Japanese newcomers—most of them men—filled that void in the national workforce. Like their Chinese predecessors, thousands of Japanese worked in railroad yards or in Pacific Coast orchards, vineyards, and berry fields. But these fiercely independent people had few illusions. They had watched as the Chinese became ostracized in American society, and while they admired the United States and hoped to financially thrive there, many planned on returning to Japan once they had made their fortunes. These men—known as *dekasegi*—were mostly bachelors or had left their families in Japan. Their US stay remained, at least in their minds, a temporary one.

By 1910 Japanese men outnumbered Japanese women in the United States by five to one. Thousands of men had returned home, but Japanese-language newspapers were now urging the *dekasegi* to stay and build a life in America. Those who did, known as *Issei*, or "first generation," soon developed their own communities. These remained separate from wider American culture. "It was a community within a community," says Japanese American Jean Nakatani Yego. "We had our own banks. We had our own churches. We had our own doctors. There was a section we weren't allowed to go out of."[4]

When Issei workers did leave their small enclaves, they were typically met with prejudice and hostility. American unions restricted the employment of the Japanese; consequently, to feed their families many of them became commercial fishermen or truck farmers who grew produce to sell. They filled a void that white farmers did not inhabit, but to do so they had to toil without sophisticated farm tools such as tractors and irrigation systems because they could not afford them. The land they tilled was often swampy, dry, or otherwise unsuitable for agriculture, but in time the Issei nourished and farmed rice fields and citrus groves into valuable plots of land. "They played a vital part in establishing the present system of marketing fruits and vegetables, especially in Los Angeles County," says historian Masakazu Iwata. "From the per-

Farmworkers of Japanese ancestry pack broccoli on California's central coast in 1937. Earlier immigrants from Japan, many of whom began arriving in the United States in the late 1880s, often found work in farming.

spective of history, it is evident that the contributions of the Issei . . . were undeniably a significant factor in making California one of the greatest farming states in the nation."[5]

Suspicion, Exclusion, and Segregation

The hard work of the Issei made little difference to the broader population. Even though many white Americans were themselves immigrants, they refused to accept the Japanese as part of their society. Jealousy and resentment festered among Issei competitors. In 1900 San Francisco mayor James Duval Phelan spoke publicly about what he perceived

Immigration Act of 1924

One of the most restrictive laws in US history was the Immigration Act of 1924. Thousands of immigrants from all over the world were streaming through Ellis Island in New York in the early 1920s. Newspapers published stories describing the chaotic influx. Americans worried that these hordes of new people might steal their jobs and undermine their way of life. In 1920 Congressman Albert Johnson visited Ellis Island and was appalled. He vowed to restrict immigration. "The country does not realize the menace of immigration," Johnson said.

Initially, Johnson promoted a two-year ban on immigration of any kind. When that measure failed, Senator William Dillingham suggested implementing a quota system that allowed in 5 percent of the number of foreign-born people already living in the country. Johnson signed on to Dillingham's plan but negotiated the quota down to 3 percent. In 1921 President Woodrow Wilson refused to sign the bill, but Johnson was undeterred. In 1924 both houses of Congress signed the Immigration Act of 1924, which limited the quota to 2 percent of those already living in the United States, according to the 1890 census. The effect of what became known as the Johnson-Reed Act was immediate and dramatic: Between 1900 and 1910, two hundred thousand Italians immigrated to the United States; the 1924 law cut that number to four thousand, a 90 percent drop. Another provision of the law prevented Asian immigrants who were ineligible to become citizens from entering the United States. The legislation remained in place until 1965.

Quoted in Vincent J. Cannato, *American Passage: The History of Ellis Island.* New York: Harper-Collins, 2010, p. 332.

as the threat of continued Japanese immigration. He also referenced earlier laws meant to prevent more Chinese from entering the United States. "The Japanese are starting the same tide of immigration which we thought we had checked twenty years ago," said Phelan. "Personally, we have nothing against the Japanese, but as they will not assimilate with us and their social life is different from ours, let them keep a respectful distance."[6]

This demand for continued segregation between Westerners and Asians was heavily promoted by a number of West Coast newspapers beginning in 1905. The *San Francisco Chronicle*, in particular, stoked the flames of resentment and fear against the Issei. Nearly every day, Americans were greeted with sensational headlines warning of an Asian invasion and Japanese spies watching people's every move. In March 1905 the California State Legislature introduced a resolution asking Congress to limit Japanese immigration. Two months later, representatives from sixty-seven local organizations united to form the Asiatic Exclusion League, a San Francisco–based group. The league's members were mostly local business owners who felt threatened by the Japanese immigrants. In only three short years the group's ranks swelled to over one hundred thousand. Working with labor unions in California to bar Asian membership in those unions, the league also promoted the boycotting of Japanese-owned restaurants and the denial of citizenship to all Asians. That same year California passed anti-miscegenation laws, barring marriage between Asians and whites.

In October 1906 the San Francisco school board announced a broad new policy: Japanese children were no longer allowed to attend the city's primary schools. Instead, they would be required to enroll in a segregated school for Chinese children in the city's Chinatown section. This policy, when published in newspapers in Tokyo, Japan, enraged the Japanese. A long-held treaty agreement with the United States promised rights of residence and educational opportunities in both countries, but the controversial school board policy appeared to deny those opportunities. The scandal forced US president Theodore Roosevelt to take action. Roosevelt was well aware of the anti-Japanese sentiment rising in the United States, and one month after the school board's announcement, he spoke directly about the issue: "To shut [the Japanese] out from the public schools is a wicked absurdity. . . . I recommend to the Congress that an act be passed specifically providing for the naturalization of Japanese who come here intending to become American citizens."[7]

"Yellow Peril"

Roosevelt's position may have been inspired less by his sympathy for Japanese immigrants than his understanding of Japan's military strength. Between February 1904 and September 1905, Japan and Russia had battled for domination of Korea and Manchuria in the Russo-Japanese War. Japan was victorious, and Roosevelt believed he could not afford to anger the Empire of Japan in an unstable part of the world.

Thus, during the months ahead the president worked on what became known as the Gentlemen's Agreement. By 1908 it was fully in place and included the repeal of the San Francisco school segregation decision. For its part, Japan agreed to restrict Japanese immigration into the United States by putting a moratorium on workers' passports.

Although the Gentlemen's Agreement calmed Americans' fears of losing their jobs to Japanese immigrants, noted scholars continued to publish articles and books about what they considered the Japanese menace not only in the United States but throughout the world. Religious leaders also wondered aloud which of the two races, white or Asian, would gain the upper hand and dominate the other. "The race question is between the colored races of the world and the white race," writes evangelical Christian pastor G.G. Rupert in his popular 1911 book *The Yellow Peril*. "Who will rule the world?"[8]

In 1919 this kind of intolerance led to the formation of the Oriental Exclusion League, which counted mainstream groups, including the American Legion, the California Federation of Labor, and the Native Sons and Daughters of the Golden West, as members. The league wanted to end Japanese immigration and deny citizenship not only to those who had immigrated but to their children, most of whom had been born in the United States.

Issei Marriage

While government action and outright prejudice slowed the flood of Issei into the United States, it contained a loophole that would prove decisive. While Japanese men were barred from further immigration, the Gentlemen's Agreement did allow Japanese wives and children into the country. For those Issei still unmarried, the agreement enabled them to marry women from Japan and bring them into the United States.

Between 1905 and 1920 thousands of young Japanese women traveled to the United States to unite with their new husbands, many of whom could not afford the trip to Japan themselves. Instead, the parents of Issei men played matchmaker. Carefully studying and interviewing potential wives for their sons abroad, the parents would make

Members of Congress look over passports of Japanese women arriving in California in 1920 to join their new husbands. Many such marriages were arranged by family members back in Japan.

suggestions and send pictures. If an Issei man liked what he saw, he might mail his own photograph to the young woman he was interested in. If the terms of marriage were mutually agreed upon by the young couple and their parents, a ceremony would be performed with a male relative standing in for the faraway Issei groom.

Once legally wed to her new husband, a picture bride packed her bags and sailed for the United States and an uncertain future. Reactions varied once husband and wife finally met. Many Issei found their wives less attractive in person than they had been in their photographs. Brides, meanwhile, had been promised lives and riches that, in the end, their husbands could not deliver.

In some cases couples quickly filed for divorce, with many of the brides returning home. Ellen Fuchida's parents were one such couple. Although Fuchida's parents ultimately remained together, their marriage got off to a difficult start. Her father made unrealistic promises to her mother before they were married, and the stark reality of life in America took an emotional toll on the young bride. "She cried for six months," says Fuchida, "but she was a very strong woman. She decided to make the best of it after she found out she was pregnant. She worked hard all of her life."[9]

As a young girl, Miwako Rosenthal learned that her father immigrated to the United States at the age of sixteen. He eventually opened a small business, and after establishing himself, he wrote home to his parents in Japan asking if they might help him find a wife with whom he could start a family. The woman who eventually arrived was smart, talented, and deeply versed in Japanese tradition. "My mother," says Rosenthal, "went to college in Japan and studied how to be a good housewife. That's the way the education system was for women in those days. They had to be socially acceptable in all forms of the cultural arts like tea ceremony."[10] The marriage between Rosenthal's parents survived and even thrived, despite the fact that they began their lives together as complete strangers.

Second Generation: Nisei

The picture bride phenomenon continued until March 1, 1920, when the Japanese government, bowing to pressure from exclusionist groups

Japanese American Citizens League

Formed in 1929 to protect the constitutional rights of Japanese Americans, the Japanese American Citizens League (JACL) began as a response to racist organizations like the Grange and Native Sons of the Golden West. Early leaders had little money and less experience in taking on government agencies and local hate groups, but like the National Association for the Advancement of Colored People, the JACL committed itself early on to fighting for civil rights. Despite its name, the California-based JACL welcomed people of all Asian races, including Chinese Americans.

In the immediate aftermath of Pearl Harbor, the JACL advised its members to submit to Executive Order 9066 peacefully, a stand which many Asian Americans harshly criticized. In the internment camps, tensions between JACL members and the general population increased: At the Tule Lake facility, group members supported government-imposed rules and regulations and labeled their more defiant fellow prisoners as troublemakers. For these reasons the JACL was often viewed as aiding the government rather than the imprisoned Japanese Americans.

Despite these conflicts, the JACL also lobbied the Roosevelt administration to allow Japanese Americans to serve in the military. After the war the JACL fought to repeal laws limiting the rights of Asians, and in 1970 the group led the first major effort for recognition of the injustice of internment. In 1994 the JACL became the first national civil rights organization to support marriage equality for all people. Today, the JACL remains committed to fairness under the law for all Americans.

in the United States, stopped the popular practice by denying passports to Japanese women. More than twenty thousand still unmarried Issei protested Japan's action, but an era had ended. Those couples already wed began forging lives together, and in time many produced children. Consequently, the Gentlemen's Agreement did not succeed in decreasing the numbers of Japanese in America; instead, growing Issei families only swelled the Japanese population in the country.

As a result, rumors and urban legends caused a minor hysteria among white Americans, many of whom now believed that before long the Japanese would outnumber them. Adding to these racist fears was a simple and immutable fact: The children of the Issei, known as Nisei, or first generation born in the United States, were automatically American citizens. According to the Fourteenth Amendment to the Constitution, "All persons born or naturalized in the United States, and subject to the jurisdiction thereof, are citizens of the United States and of the state wherein they reside."[11]

Therefore, while the Issei were forced to abide by American law as it related to immigrants, their sons and daughters were to be accorded the full rights of citizenship long denied to their mothers and fathers. This more permanent connection to the United States also had a practical legal effect on the Issei and their families. Before, they were often barred from purchasing land to farm; now, Issei could buy land by naming their children as owners and signing on as legal guardians until the children were old enough to take full command of the property.

While the Issei remained steeped in Japanese traditions, the Nisei came of age in American culture; they attended public schools and pledged allegiance not to Japan but to the United States. Most spoke Japanese at home, yet English was their primary language. They listened to American music and dressed in American clothes, but they inherited many of their parents' values and recognized from an early age that they were different.

Caught in the Middle

This feeling of not quite belonging extended to virtually all aspects of Nisei life. Much like African Americans at the time, these young Japanese Americans were often barred from movie theaters, restaurants, swimming pools, school functions such as dances, and other public places. This blatant discrimination angered many of them, but others became self-conscious and insecure, sometimes blaming themselves or their families for the racism aimed at them.

Some teenage Nisei were already embarrassed by their parents' traditions, but a desire to fit in with young, white Americans only made matters worse. "I was ashamed of [my father] . . . for being so unalterably Japanese," says California native Jeanne Wakatsuki Houston. "I would not bring home my friends for fear of what he would say or do."[12] Some even believed that to be respected within the Nisei community they had to rebel against their old-world parents; after all, it was their parents' ethnicity and, in turn, their own, that made them outsiders even in the country of their birth. One young Nisei named Ichiro spoke honestly and openly about his own sense of youthful self-hatred: "No matter how much I look in the mirror, I cannot change; it is the same old Ichiro—my face is that of an Oriental. I want to be a Caucasian, accepted and comfortable, but when I look at myself honestly, I must face the painful reality that I am a Japanese, a member of a minority group which I reject, and I hate it."[13]

Many of the Nisei self-segregated, avoiding contact with white classmates. Such behavior made them seem all the more suspicious to their peers. To combat these feelings of inferiority, some Nisei, encouraged by their parents, worked even harder to excel, especially in school. "I can recall our parents telling us we had to do well in school because we would have to be twice as good as the next student in order to get jobs, get an education," says Nisei and former soldier Sam Ozaki. "We were well aware that we were not white."[14] Others joined civic organizations, determined to prove their loyalty to the United States. One popular group, the Japanese American Citizens League (JACL), dismayed many Issei. They saw the JACL as a fringe group bent on erasing proud Japanese traditions. The JACL's creed read in part, "I am proud that I am an American citizen of Japanese ancestry, for my very background makes me appreciate more fully the wonderful advantages of this nation."[15]

Japanese Imperialism

Issei and their Nisei children continued hoping that they would eventually be more accepted into American society, but by 1939 the nation and much of the world had more immediate concerns. In August, German chancellor Adolf Hitler secured the Soviet Union's promise that the two countries would remain allies. Less than a month later, on September 1, Hitler's Nazi troops invaded Poland; Great Britain and France consequently declared war on Germany. The growing conflict in Europe threatened to spread across the world, but the United States

A resident of Hollywood, California, makes sure that no one mistakes her feelings about Japanese immigrants in 1923. Signs like this one were not unique to California during a time when many Americans feared being outnumbered by Japanese newcomers.

and its president, Franklin D. Roosevelt, worked to remain neutral. Yet the nation's fragile relationship with the Empire of Japan soon threatened to change the nature of World War II and forever transform the fate of the Japanese living in the United States.

The diplomatic relationship between Japan and the United States had never been warm. The rapport between the starkly different nations and cultures was further frayed by Japan's imperial ambitions in the 1930s. In September 1931 Japanese forces invaded Manchuria. Even more dramatic and deadly was the empire's violent invasion of mainland China in July 1937. In the city of Shanghai alone, the nearly four months of brutal fighting and killing led to the deaths of between 100,000 and 250,000 Chinese men, women, and children. Forty thousand Japanese troops were killed.

In late September 1940 Japan advanced on French Indochina, present-day Vietnam, as a way of stopping China from importing arms, ammunition, and oil through that country. For decades the United States had retained military and economic might in the Pacific region and now attempted to convince Japanese forces to withdraw from Manchuria and China by leveling economic sanctions on Japan. Faced with stifling shortages of much-needed oil and other natural resources, Japan made a fateful decision. On September 27, 1940, Japan's leaders signed the Tripartite Pact with Germany and Italy. By doing so, Japan joined a military alliance known as the Axis.

Like its German ally, Japan also signed a neutrality agreement with the Soviet Union as a way of preventing an attack by the Soviets if Japan chose to attack the United States or Great Britain. The international pressure on all parties continued in July 1941 when authorities from the United States and Netherlands moved to freeze Japan's financial assets in response to Japan's occupation of southern Indochina. Yet despite its desperate need for oil to fuel its tanks and other military hardware, the Asian empire refused to back down, even after direct calls by the United States for Japan to withdraw from China and Indochina.

On September 6 Japanese leaders held an imperial conference and decided that if negotiations with authorities in Washington did not lead to a breakthrough, Japan would have no choice but to declare war on the United States, Great Britain, and Netherlands. Neither Japan's emperor Hirohito nor many of his naval officers believed war was the best course, but they deferred to the militant generals of their supreme command.

American military commanders, meanwhile, echoed the unease among many white Americans over Japanese imperialism. Closer to home, they also feared that the Japanese living in the United States might become collaborators with the Empire of Japan. Before long, a surprise attack and the rush to war forever changed the lives of Japanese Americans.

Chapter 2

War and Evacuation

In a letter dated October 15, 1941, US president Franklin D. Roosevelt voiced his deep concern over the state of affairs with Japan to British prime minister Winston Churchill: "The Jap situation is definitely worse," he wrote, "and I think they are headed north."[16] By then tension over the oil embargo and Japan's continued quest to conquer most of Asia had come to a boil. Yet what Roosevelt could neither predict nor stop was an early morning attack that altered the course of American history and led irrevocably to the internment of Japanese Americans.

March to War

Japanese leaders began to prepare for war in early November 1941. Still, they agreed to continue negotiations to try to avoid conflict with the United States and its allies. To that end, Japan sent Ambassador Kichisaburō Nomura and emissary Saburō Kurusu to Washington, DC, to present two plans to the Roosevelt administration.

Plan A asked the United States to fully accept Japan's imperial ambitions in Asia. When US authorities rejected this offer, Nomura and Kurusu presented Plan B, which called for both Japan and the United States to avoid sending troops into Southeast Asia, except for Indochina, which Japanese troops already occupied. It also called for a restoration of trade between the two nations, including a suspension of the oil embargo. American authorities rejected this plan, too.

A US counterproposal, made on November 26, called for Japan to withdraw from both China and Indochina and reject the Tripartite

Pact with Germany and the Soviet Union. American secretary of state Cordell Hull suspected that what he proposed would likely be rebuffed by Japan and that war would be the likely outcome. But he told Secretary of War Henry L. Stimson he would consider the matter no longer, saying: "I have washed my hands of it, and it is now in the hands of you and [Secretary of the Navy Frank] Knox."[17]

Surprise Attack

The US Army and Navy were unprepared for war in the Pacific and needed at least three months to get ready, but time ran out. The largest American military base in the Pacific region was Pearl Harbor, located on the island of Oahu in Hawaii. In the early morning hours of December 7, 1941, two on-duty radar operators noticed something strange on their screens. It was, they later said, "completely out of the ordinary."[18] Although the men had to check twice to believe it, their instruments told them that two large groups of airplanes were 132 miles (212 km) from where they sat and were rapidly heading in their direction.

In the coming hours, 353 Japanese bombers, fighters, and torpedo planes launched from six aircraft carriers in the Pacific swooped down on Pearl Harbor. Thousands of Americans ran for their lives as wave after wave rained down death, destruction, and terror. Panic-stricken sailors did their best to defend themselves, but their efforts were overwhelmed by the intense and all-consuming Japanese bombardment. "There were a lot of explosions," remembers one sailor whose name is not recorded. "The worst part was you couldn't see anything. You could hear and feel the explosions. You didn't know what was going on."[19]

Once the many fires had been doused and the smoke cleared, the toll became apparent: four American battleships, including the USS *Arizona*, had been sunk; four more were badly damaged. One hundred eighty-eight US aircraft were completely destroyed. Twenty-four hundred American servicemen along with civilians, were dead. The following day, at a joint session of Congress, Roosevelt delivered the stirring "Day of Infamy" speech that led Congress to immediately declare war on Japan.

Response and Reprisal

The response of Japanese Americans to the attack on Pearl Harbor was swift and unequivocal. Organizations like the JACL almost immediately released statements condemning what they saw as Japan's unprovoked aggression and reiterating their loyalty to the United States: "We in our hearts know we are Americans—loyal to America," writes the JACL in a telegram to the White House. "We must prove that to all of you."[20]

Despite such statements, war abroad meant increased conflict at home for Issei and Nisei, many of whom began suffering discrimination more directly than ever before. Kaname (Ken) Takemoto, a twenty-one-year-old sophomore at the University of Hawaii, had witnessed the attack on Pearl Harbor from outside his dorm room. Now he saw firsthand how public sentiment was turning against people who looked like he did.

Editorials in Hawaii's newspapers called for placing local Japanese people in concentration camps or deporting them from the islands. But such a policy was hardly feasible in Hawaii, where more than a third of the workforce was Japanese—more than 157,000 people. Still, some restrictions were put in place, especially those related to the military on Oahu.

Japanese members of the university's Reserve Officers' Training Corps (ROTC), including Takemoto, were discharged from the program and not allowed to use or carry guns or ammunition. The young men were all reclassified as 4C, or "enemy alien." They were no longer considered trustworthy. "All of this came as a shock," says Takemoto. "I had never encountered racial prejudice before. But now there was an immediate stigma to being Japanese."[21]

Issei Under Suspicion

American officials feared a Japanese attack on the mainland's West Coast and vowed to keep an eye on anyone of Japanese descent. The Issei found themselves in a precarious position with respect to their loyalty. They were not citizens of the United States, as their children were, and many of them retained ties to Japan as members of patriotic groups, most of which swore devotion to the Empire of the Sun, as Japan was known. Fearing reprisal, including arrest, many Issei destroyed any artifacts from their country of birth. This included copies of Japanese newspapers, books, and flags—anything they believed authorities might find suspicious.

Issei fears became reality in the hours after the attack on Pearl Harbor. In the summer of 1940 the US Congress had passed the Alien Registration Act, a law that required all aliens over the age of fourteen to register with the government. Meanwhile, the US Department of Justice gathered names of people who it believed posed a potential threat to US security. In the wake of Pearl Harbor, agents from the Federal Bureau of Investigation (FBI) began arresting and questioning three thousand men deemed to be subversive and dangerous. Half of these were Japanese. The other half consisted of German and Italian immigrants because the United States was also now at war with Germany and Italy, the two others members of the Axis powers.

The FBI agents showed up unannounced at all hours of the day or night and ordered the Japanese men they were looking for to come with them. "They just ransacked our entire house," says Nisei artist Bessie Masuda. "They went through everything, and we didn't know what was going on. And then my mom is crying, and then I start crying. We all cried. Then they said to my dad that he would have to go with them. And they told him to just bring his toothbrush."[22]

Most of those taken away were leaders in their Issei communities or kept some of their money in Japanese banks. Others were commercial fishermen who federal authorities feared could signal to enemy ships off the California coast. The whereabouts of those detained were kept secret, but nearly all were transferred to internment camps run by the Justice Department around the United States.

Fifth Column Fear

Panic quickly set in. Rumors and hearsay led to genuine fear that another attack from Japan was imminent. Old reports resurfaced about spies from Tokyo attempting to contaminate the food and water supply in the United States. FBI director J. Edgar Hoover ordered his agents to

Niihau Incident

In the days after the attack on Pearl Harbor, an episode known as the Niihau Incident stoked American fears. On the morning of December 7, Japanese pilot Shigenori Nishikaichi crash-landed his bullet-riddled plane on the Hawaiian island of Niihau. Native Hawaiian Hawila Kaleohano had not yet heard about the attack, yet recognizing the plane as Japanese, he took the dazed airman's pistol and identification papers and put him under guard. Kaleohano sent for Yoshio Harada, a Hawaiian-born man of Japanese ancestry, so that Harada could interpret for the young pilot. Nishikaichi quietly asked Harada and another Japanese man for help, and soon after, the three overpowered Nishikaichi's guards and escaped.

For six days the armed airman and his accomplices roamed the island looking for the pilot's identification papers. On December 13 the hungry and desperate renegades took a local man, Ben Kanahele, and his wife, Ella, hostage. When Nishikaichi threatened to kill Ella, Ben reached for his captor's shotgun; the pilot drew a pistol from his boot and fired, hitting Ben three times. Ella, meanwhile, picked up a heavy rock and smashed the pilot's skull with it. Her husband, wounded but not fatally, cut Nishikaichi's throat, killing him. Harada, the pilot's main co-conspirator, shot himself. In the aftermath of the episode, Ben Kanahele was awarded the Purple Heart and Medal of Merit for his bravery. Still, naval Lieutenant C.B. Baldwin, author of the official Niihau report, worried that Japanese Americans "may give valuable aid to Japanese invaders in cases where the tide of battle is in favor of Japan."

Quoted in Dennis M. Ogawa, *Kodomo No Tame Ni: For the Sake of the Children*. Honolulu: University Press of Hawaii, 1978, p. 272.

investigate other national gossip, particularly a story suggesting Japanese agents planned to set massive fires in the shape of arrows as a way of guiding Japanese bombers to targets in Seattle, Washington. Hoover's men found the cause of the fires: a Seattle farmer burning brush. Such hair-trigger hysteria existed not only among American citizenry; government officials also promoted the notion of enemy attack.

On December 15, 1941, Knox fueled the public frenzy when he called Pearl Harbor "the most effective Fifth Column work of the entire war."[23] A fifth column is a secret group of people seeking to undermine or destroy a nation from within. Four days later Knox, with virtually no evidence to justify such a drastic action, strongly encouraged Roosevelt to remove all people of Japanese ancestry from Hawaii. Although US attorney general Francis Biddle believed the suspicions and the plans were outrageous and completely unfounded, Knox found a like-minded ally in Lieutenant General John L. DeWitt, chief of the army's Western Defense Command.

DeWitt, like Knox, stressed the clear and present danger of Japanese sabotage. He released a series of reports claiming that Japanese submarines were intercepting US shipping schedules, and he had the army issue an alert warning that Japanese ships were sailing toward San Francisco. Each of these claims only deepened Americans' fears, and DeWitt continued to push his agenda. In the immediate aftermath of Pearl Harbor, his Western Defense Command demanded that the FBI raid the homes of suspected Japanese spies or disloyal people to look for guns, ammunition, and radio receivers with which these subversives could communicate with officials in Japan.

After carrying out these searches and seizures, the Department of Justice rendered its judgment: "We have not found a single machine gun nor have we found any gun in any circumstances indicating that it was helpful to our enemies. We have not found a camera which we have reason to believe was for use in espionage."[24]

Media Scrutiny

Despite these findings, DeWitt's push for action against Japanese Americans was echoed in much of the media. Radio commentator

The battleships USS West Virginia and USS Tennessee burn in the Japanese attack on Pearl Harbor in December 1941. Japanese American organizations immediately condemned the attack and reaffirmed the loyalty of their members to their adopted country.

John Hughes from the Mutual Broadcasting Network used his popular program to harp on the need to do something about the purported Japanese fifth column. He painted a frightening picture that fanned the flames of anti-Japanese sentiment:

> Thousands of Japanese fifth columnists are wandering around at will—or perhaps "wandering" is not the word—they know what they're doing, and what they intend to do. . . . It is all

very well to be nice to our enemies, at least to the point of recognizing that they are human beings, and worthy of humane treatment, but to give them a sort of preferred status that permits them to continue their operations against us, seems a little thick.[25]

Henry McClemore, a columnist for the Hearst newspapers, advocated sending the Japanese to the desolate and isolated Badlands of South Dakota. "Herd 'em up, pack 'em off, and give 'em the inside room of the badlands," he wrote. "Let 'em be pinched, hurt, hungry and dead up against it."[26] By early February 1942, McClemore was joined by a majority of West Coast newspapers in calling for the mass evacuation of the Japanese.

The anti-Japanese contingent also found a local ally in Earl Warren, attorney general of California, who lobbied for the removal of Japanese people from the West Coast. The collective pressure convinced Roosevelt to take broad action. On January 14, 1942, he issued Presidential Proclamation 2537, which required all aliens—not only those of Japanese heritage—to report any change of name, address, or employment to the FBI. Failure to do so could result in arrest and detainment until the war was over. This proclamation was followed one month later by an even more stringent one.

Executive Order 9066

On February 19, 1942, Roosevelt's Executive Order 9066 authorized the secretary of war to begin the selection of military commanders who would subsequently designate "military areas in such places . . . from which any or all persons may be excluded."[27] In other words, the rights of some people to move about freely would be restricted. In the wake of Executive Order 9066, Stimson recorded his own thoughts in a diary. While Stimson firmly believed that the Japanese—by nature of their race—could not be trusted, he also questioned whether Roosevelt's action was legal under the articles of the US Constitution. He wrote, "Their racial characteristics are such that we cannot understand or trust

Internment in Canada

The United States was not alone in interning people of Japanese ancestry. The nation's neighbor to the north, Canada, had its own Japanese population and, like many Americans, white Canadians were suspicious of these citizens. Twenty-two thousand of them lived in British Columbia, where they faced chronic discrimination and violence. In the days after Pearl Harbor, Canadian Pacific Railways and many other companies fired its Japanese employees. The boats of Japanese fishermen in British Columbia were confiscated by the government. "It is the government's plan to get these people out of B.C. as fast as possible," said federal cabinet minister from British Columbia Ian MacKenzie. "It is my personal intention, as long as I remain in public life, to see they never come back here. Let our slogan be for British Columbia: No Japs from the Rockies to the seas."

When two thousand Canadian soldiers were killed or imprisoned defending the island of Hong Kong on December 18, 1941, anger boiled over. Weeks later, the Canadian government created a "protected area" along its western coast and ordered the relocation of twenty-three thousand men, women, and children of Japanese ancestry. First, they spent months living in animal pens in Vancouver. Eventually, the families were separated: Men worked on road gangs; women and children were sent to live in shantytowns deep in the Canadian wilderness. Meanwhile, Canadian officials took charge of Japanese property and authorized its sale. Those imprisoned were eventually released, but they were left with nothing, and their lives were never the same.

Quoted in CBC Learning, "Japanese Internment: British Columbia Wages War Against Japanese Canadians," 2001. www.cbc.ca.

even the citizen Japanese. . . . [This] is the fact but I am afraid it will make a tremendous hole in our constitutional system."[28]

DeWitt appeared to have no such misgivings. In the aftermath of Executive Order 9066, he reiterated his belief that Japanese Americans were not to be trusted and that exclusion and perhaps detainment were appropriate ways to deal with the problem, despite any questions of legality. "A Jap's a Jap," said DeWitt. "They are a dangerous element, whether loyal or not. There is no way to determine their loyalty . . . it makes no difference whether he is an American; theoretically he is still a Japanese and you can't change him . . . by giving him a piece of paper."[29]

In March DeWitt made a dramatic announcement to the American people: All people of Japanese ancestry and other aliens would soon be excluded from what he referred to as Military Area 1. This included the western half of three states—California, Oregon, and Washington— and the southern half of Arizona. Military Area 2, he said, included what was left of those four states. There, movement was unrestricted except for so-called prohibited zones. In practice, this meant that Japanese Americans residing in the restricted areas would have to leave their homes.

While they may have felt betrayed, most of those displaced accepted their fate and calmly did their best to follow instructions. "We wanted to show the Americans that we are Americans, and that we are not dangerous people," says Kaz Fujishima, whose family members were Issei fruit farmers. "and that if this is what you want us to do we'll go along with it."[30] Still, the instructions themselves were confusing and often contradictory, even though the evacuations were referred to by government officials as "voluntary."

Nowhere to Go

The federal government's idea was to push these people away from the West Coast, where, authorities believed, they posed the largest threat to national security. But as Japanese families attempted to move to new locations in states such as Nevada, Utah, and Idaho, they found the conditions and their potential neighbors less than hospitable. Locals posted large signs and banners containing warnings such as "Japs Keep Moving" or "This restaurant poisons both rats and Japs." With nowhere else to go, many families tried to return home.

By the end of March, DeWitt began to recognize the failure of his plan and halted voluntary evacuations. He also called for the building of temporary living quarters to house evacuees. Meanwhile, on March 18 the US government established the War Relocation Authority (WRA). Its job was to take charge of nearly one hundred thousand people once they had moved from prohibited areas and to find them jobs.

As the WRA worked to organize itself, the US Army began announcing instructions for mandatory evacuation of all Japanese Americans and their families. The first such announcement appeared on March 24, 1942. These Civilian Exclusion Orders continued through June and were posted across California, Oregon, and Washington— anywhere with large Japanese populations. Soldiers and police officers typically nailed the orders to telephone poles and posted them in shop windows.

The large, bolded word *Japanese* printed on the posters was hard for anyone to miss. On closer reading, the exclusion orders advised Japanese to report to local civil control stations housed in local libraries or other municipal buildings, where they would be registered and provided an identification number. This number would remain the chief means of identifying Japanese families throughout the war. The registration center also instructed families what exactly they could bring with them when evacuated. These items included clothing, toiletries, sheets, blankets, pillows, and any personal effects. Japanese American families were quickly overwhelmed: Decisions about what to take and what to do with their homes and other possessions left many feeling frightened, angry, and desperate.

Evacuation Day

The WRA's leadership felt likewise beleaguered. Its first director, Milton Eisenhower, was replaced in June 1942 by Dillon S. Myer. Later, Myer spoke of the overwhelming task of relocating so many

Japanese. "Neither I nor most of my staff were well informed regarding the problems we faced," he says. "We lacked information about the evacuees and their history. We were generally uninformed regarding the anti-oriental movements on the West Coast, and the pressures, rumors, and fears that had led to the evacuation."[31] Despite the WRA's lack of information and its struggle to manage the growing operation, Japanese Americans had been put on notice: They were leaving.

Depending on one's location, Evacuation Day, or E-Day, came during the spring or summer months of 1942. Families arrived at their designated control stations dragging suitcases and boxes behind them. To speed the tense experience and calm nerves, volunteers from local churches lent a hand, providing coffee and doughnuts and rides for the elderly or infirm. Parents, grandparents, and children huddled together wearing identification tags and waiting for the buses or trains that would take them away. Where they would go and how long they would be gone remained a mystery. Oregon high school teacher Azalia Peet lamented the loss of some of her best students and wondered why they and their families needed to leave. "These are law-abiding, upright people of our community," she said. "What is it that makes it necessary for them to evacuate?"[32]

Assembly Centers

The evacuation of Japanese Americans from San Francisco began on April 7, 1942. That day, 644 men, women, and children were put on trains and transferred to a hastily constructed temporary camp at the Santa Anita Racetrack near Los Angeles. Later that month and into early May thousands more—almost half of San Francisco's Japanese American population—were moved to a Tanforan racetrack, twelve miles south of the city. Both facilities now closed to the general public, became centers for evacuees.

Their accommodations were cramped and filthy. Small housing units were set up in the horse stalls, all of which were divided into two rooms. Ramshackle cots and small wood-burning or kerosene stoves were the primary comforts. The summer months meant hot days and—

depending on one's location—cold nights. Crammed together for days, families could do little but survive and wait for relief. Most evacuees remained in this kind of assembly center for more than three months as they awaited more permanent accommodations.

In the first weeks of the evacuation, roughly 18,000 of the 110,000 evacuees were sent immediately to the Manzanar relocation center in southern California or the Poston center in Arizona. These two locations, the first to be completed by the WRA, served as both the permanent relocation centers and temporary assembly centers for those who would soon be sent elsewhere. Apart from these two locations, fifteen other temporary assembly centers were spread across California, Oregon, and Washington.

En route to Rohwer relocation camp in Arkansas, hundreds of people of Japanese ancestry board a train at the Santa Anita Racetrack assembly center in 1942. Many evacuees stayed in the cramped and filthy conditions of Santa Anita for months before being moved elsewhere.

Regardless of where they were, the evacuees could not help but notice that their new environment was surrounded by barbed wire fencing and that armed guards watched their every move. At night searchlights scanned the ground surrounding their tiny living spaces, looking for anyone trying to escape. Meanwhile, the cities and small towns the Japanese left behind hardly missed them. Indeed, on May 21, 1942, the *San Francisco Chronicle* reported a stark fact: The Japanese were gone. "For the first time in 81 years," the paper said, "not a single Japanese is walking the streets of San Francisco."[33]

The temporary assembly centers were, for many, only the first stop on a perilous journey into the unknown. While some American voices cried out for justice, most of them went unheard. The ordeal for these loyal but frightened Japanese American families was only beginning.

Chapter 3

Life in Camps

A few months after the attack on Pearl Harbor, President Franklin D. Roosevelt again wrote to British prime minister Winston Churchill. He reflected on the ongoing war and the challenges caused by Japan's actions. He also vowed that American retribution was only in its early stages. "The injuries that all of us have suffered at the hands of Japan are indeed grievous," he told Churchill. "A partial retribution in kind has been meted out to the Japanese forces during the last seven months. This is only the beginning."[34] At that very moment, more than 110,000 Nisei and Issei found themselves at the start of their own odyssey. Forty percent of these were children; 70 percent were American citizens. Unlike the American president they were virtually helpless, and fighting back appeared futile. World War II raged in the Pacific and in Europe, but these Japanese Americans remained trapped by discrimination and detention in their own country.

Transfer and Arrival

In June 1942, after weeks of being stuck in assembly centers, evacuated Japanese Americans began the exhausting and difficult journey to newly completed WRA relocation camps. The idea was simple: Move them as far from the nation's large cities as possible. In building these permanent sites, the WRA followed four principal guidelines: Although the locations would be relatively remote, they had to be accessible to public utilities such as water and power; none could be built near military bases or large cities; each had to have the potential to hold no less than five thousand people; and all camps were to be located on federal land.

Part of the WRA's plan for the ten permanent internment camps included agricultural development and arable land on which internees could farm. Yet most of the final location sites were not conducive to farming. Rohwer and Jerome in Arkansas were swampy; Manzanar in California and Gila River in Arizona were located in dry, desert-like areas. The largest camp, Tule Lake in California, provided the most potential for cultivating crops because of the rich soil that surrounded its dry lake bed.

The future residents of the camps, meanwhile, again boarded trains and buses. The journey by rail, which could take days, tested the patience and resilience of even the heartiest evacuees. But for the youngest among them, traveling far from home at least held the possibility of excitement. "At the time, at twelve years old, you might call it an adventure," says Nob Kamibayashi, who traveled to Manzanar as a boy. "You are going somewhere where you haven't been before. You don't know what's there and so it was kind of a surprise adventure, [even though we were] scared and had kind of mixed emotions."[35] As the hours passed, though, initial excitement turned to boredom and boredom to exhaustion. One day bled into another. Passengers were thirsty and hungry; they had no idea where they were headed. As the sun rose on another day, conditions began to deteriorate. The summer heat made many of the trips virtually unbearable. "It was all cramped and hot," says Japanese American Sam Mibu. "We couldn't go anywhere, and we had to sleep sitting up, and it actually was torture."[36]

Victor Muraoka was a child of nine when he and his family boarded a train to Manzanar. He remembers hearing rumors about their final destination. "Somewhere along the way, either before we got to the camp or when we arrived, I heard some people talking and someone said that we would be in camp the rest of our lives," he says. "I believed it."[37]

Momo Nagano entered the Manzanar internment camp as a sixteen-year-old, but the place that she had imagined before she arrived was starkly different than the reality that confronted her. "I had envisioned Manzanar as a camp of little white cottages for each

Internment Camps and Assembly Centers

○ War Relocation Centers   ▲ Assembly Centers   ▨ Exclusion Zone

Puyallup ▲ WA
Portland ▲
OR
ID
Tule Lake ○   Minidoka ○   ○ Heart Mtn.
CA   WY
Marysville
▲ Sacramento
Tanforan ▲   ▲ Stockton   ○ Topaz
Salinas ▲   ▲ Turlock   UT   CO
Pinedale   ▲ Merced
Fresno   ▲ Owens Valley   Granada ○
Tulare   ○ Manzanar   AZ
Santa Anita   ▲ Pomona   ▲ Mayer   AR
Poston ○   ○ Rohwer
Parker Dam   ○ Jerome
○ Gila River

Note: The exclusion zone was created under a presidential executive order allowing local military commanders to designate zones that excluded anyone of Japanese ancestry.

family, like the ones at Sequoia National Park where we had stayed during vacations," she says. "I can still vividly recall my dismay as we pulled into Manzanar . . . and saw rows of black tarpapered barracks, some . . . still being built."[38]

Not Welcome

Most internment camps were located away from populated areas in some of the most remote and isolated parts of the United States. Not so those built in Jerome and Rohwer, Arkansas. As the trains carrying Japanese Americans and their extended families arrived in Jerome, hundreds of

Clara Breed: Camp Lifeline

From 1929 to 1945, Clara Breed worked as a children's book librarian at San Diego's Central Library. There she encountered many young Japanese Americans. As they and their families were being rounded up, Miss Breed, as the children knew her, gave each of them a packet of stamped postcards; this way they could remain in touch with her. Before long, Breed was mailing them candy, clothes, and books, as well as writing letters of support for fathers detained and located away from their families. Many of the letters sent to Breed from the camps describe hardships—long lines for showers and food—yet they also contain joy and a determination to survive. The young people express their gratitude for the gifts that Breed sent them. "Dear Miss Breed," reads one from twenty-two-year-old Tetsuzo Hirasaki, "You should have seen the looks of pleasure on the faces of our friends with whom we were able to share the candy and nuts. . . . Receiving things from the outside is such a rarity that most of us share what we receive no matter how little it is." Breed kept all 250 letters and cards sent to her and in the early 1990s gave them to one of her former students, Elizabeth Yamada. When Breed died in 1994 Yamada donated the documents to the Japanese American National Museum in Los Angeles.

Tetsuzo Hirasaki, "Letter from Tetsuzo (Ted) Hirasaki," Collections and Research, Japanese American National Museum, December 1, 1942. www.janm.org.

people—both white and black—stood to watch. Yet they were not there to welcome the new arrivals; instead, they came to get a look at the strangers who would be living among them.

Like so many Americans, these small-town residents brought a knee-jerk prejudice to all things Japanese. Not only was their nation at war with Japan, but the looks and culture of Japanese Americans were unlike anything they had experienced before. "There was a lot of fear in both communities," remembers Rohwer resident Richard Smith. "People saw any Japanese person as the enemy. We feared everything that was Japanese."[39] With the sudden influx of internees, Jerome and Rohwer quickly became the fifth and sixth largest cities in the state.

Before long, resentment festered among the local population. Rumors swirled that those imprisoned were receiving the kinds of prized food—ham, bacon, fruit—that they themselves could not get because of food rationing. Camp schools and hospitals also became the subject of hostility among many Arkansans. "They were given a hospital, which we didn't have," says Jerome resident Frances Hopmann. "They had nice schools, which we had to travel a good ways to go to school. And it seemed like there was always some little something that they could get that we couldn't. And that's what kept the anger and the people all in an uproar."[40] When Nisei men and women were allowed to venture into Jerome or Rohrer, they were met with anger and prejudice.

Camp Conditions

West of Arkansas, the largest camp, California's Tule Lake, eventually housed 18,789 people. Granada, in Colorado, was the smallest, with only 7,318 residents. Constructed by the US Army, the camp barracks resembled standard military housing of the time and were made of pinewood planks. Barracks, which measured 20 by 100 to 120 feet (6 by 30 to 37 m), were divided into four or six rooms; each of these measured 20 by 16 feet (6 by 5 m) to 20 by 25 feet (6 by 8 m). Each room housed one family, regardless of the family's size, and contained a coal stove, army cots, mattresses, and blankets. As families arrived many windows had not yet been installed, thus offering little protection from the elements.

Every long barracks block housed approximately sixty families, along with mess hall, laundry, and shower facilities. Lack of privacy proved particularly trying. "That was the hardest thing to get used to," says Ruth Yonemoto, who was a teenager at the time. "There's a stall with about ten or fifteen shower heads, and there you are having to go take a shower, so we used to wait until about three o'clock in the morning. Circumstances were very humiliating."[41]

The camps were overcrowded; bathroom conditions were, by most accounts, unsanitary. Traditional Japanese ideas of modesty and dignity quickly met the harsh reality of life in camp. Some adapted, while others had a harder time. "Like so many women there, Mama never did get used to the latrines," writes Jeanne Wakatsuki Houston, whose family spent time at Manzanar. "It was a humiliation she just learned to endure: *shikata ga nai*, this cannot be helped."[42]

In 1943 the WRA published a report about the circumstances in which the internees were forced to live. The housing was described this way: "Tarpaper-covered barracks of simple frame construction without plumbing or any cooking facilities of any kind."[43] At night, such meager shelter proved trying for those imprisoned. Depending on a camp's location and the time of year, the nights could be chilly or freezing. But even on the coldest nights coal for a family's stove was scarce, and most had no choice but to huddle under their government-issued wool blankets.

As it was in the world outside the camps, food was rationed because of the war. The WRA spent roughly forty-eight cents per person per day feeding the internees, a small amount even in the 1940s. The mess halls held 250 to 300 people, who were served by their fellow prisoners. When it came to food, though, experiences from camp to camp could vary widely. Artist Kango Takamura spent his internment at Manzanar, where provisions were plentiful. The camp, he said, "had plenty of food . . . not gourmet stuff, but good enough for health."[44]

The camps were run by WRA staff members, many of whom brought their families, including children, with them. Although these white teachers and administrators lived within the boundaries of the camps, the two groups rarely interacted. "We lived inside the fence, with nothing to separate us from the Japanese, but did not often mingle," says Art Williams, whose father worked as assistant chief of internal security at Manzanar. Fourteen when he arrived, Williams remained mostly in the WRA staff areas. "I felt comfortable in my little part of camp," he says, "but not in theirs. It was like a force field separating us. It was not there to see, but it could be felt."[45]

Internees sent to relocation camps such as Manzanar (pictured) in California's desolate Owens Valley lived in basic military-style barracks. In some camps, barracks were divided into four to six rooms with one family in each room.

Daily Life

A sense of separation also plagued the internees. Like the assembly centers, camps were surrounded by barbed wire, and guards with machine guns were posted in towers nearby. The US Army remained in charge of security for each camp, controlling who came and went. The tension between guards and residents sometimes led to injuries or death. In early 1943 at Manzanar, Hikoji Takeuchi walked outside the center of camp to collect wood and was shot by a guard. Takeuchi survived. In April 1943 at Topaz camp near Delta, Utah, sixty-three-year-old Hatsuki Wakasa walked toward an outer fence. A guard who believed the man was trying to escape commanded him to stop. Wakasa kept moving; the guard fired, killing him.

Although all of the residents were there because they shared a common ethnicity, they varied in their religious beliefs, upbringing, and social status. The camps housed Buddhists as well as Christians, city

The 100th and 442nd

When Japanese bombers attacked Pearl Harbor in 1941, more than five thousand Japanese Americans were already enlisted in the US armed forces. Although most were discharged in the panic that followed, some Nisei volunteers remained determined to fight for their country. Beginning in May 1942 hundreds of them joined the 100th Infantry Battalion stationed in Hawaii. Less than a year later, in January 1943, the War Department created a segregated unit, the 442nd Regimental Combat Team, consisting of Hawaiian Nisei and Japanese American soldiers from the mainland.

By June 1943, at the height of the war, the 100th was on its way to North Africa. There, the battalion fought the Nazis alongside the 34th Division. Later that year, the battalion was sent to Italy, where it saw fierce combat and suffered high casualties, thereby earning the nickname the "Purple Heart Battalion." In June 1944 the 100th was incorporated into the 442nd. By the war's end, the 100th/442nd was one of the most decorated units in the American military, with eighteen thousand individuals earning awards for bravery, ninety-five hundred of them Purple Hearts. In 2010 President Barack Obama awarded the Japanese American veterans the Congressional Gold Medal for their distinguished service. "While some Japanese Americans were being wrongly interned due only to their ethnicity, these brave men stepped forward to defend our nation," said Hawaii senator Daniel Akaka. "Their bravery helped to not only win the war, it paved the way towards a more tolerant and just nation."

CNN, "Japanese-American Army Units from World War II Honored," October 5, 2010. www.cnn.com.

dwellers along with country folk, rich and poor alike. Now they lived together in one community in which they all had to get along and survive. The WRA had ultimate responsibility for what happened to these people, but they allowed each camp to participate in some of the decision making by encouraging them to form resident councils.

Each block of fourteen barracks elected a "blockhead" whose job was to listen to and record grievances among the internees. These were then passed on to WRA leaders. In practice, the blockheads and resident councils had little power, with their overseers often choosing to ignore camp problems. To control the camps the WRA enlisted the help of Nisei men and women. Officials remained distrustful of the older generation of Japanese. This promotion of the younger people, however, fomented resentment among their parents and grandparents.

Work and Play

WRA authorities put camp residents to work as a way of keeping them occupied and maintaining the camps. Unskilled internees were paid sixteen dollars per month to keep the camps clean or wash dishes in the mess hall. Doctors, teachers, or other educated professionals received nineteen dollars. If a camp was located near a populated area, workers could apply for passes that allowed them to work in nearby towns. In Arkansas, however, despite a labor shortage, the governor refused to allow Japanese youth to work in the state. Consequently, the young people soon applied to work elsewhere, both to escape camp life and to help support their families. After detailed security checks, more than thirty-six thousand Nisei left their parents to work as secretaries and clerks.

Men, who often depended on their work outside the home to give them a sense of purpose and accomplishment, often became depressed. The elderly, too, sometimes succumbed to periods of melancholy. Despite the hardships, however, internees found ways to make life bearable. They had no choice. To fight these feelings of hopelessness families worked to create living spaces of color and beauty. Some fashioned beautiful gardens out of the harsh desert landscape. Others polished sagebrush roots they found to create gorgeous natural sculptures.

To help the internees pass the time, camp directors organized frequent church services, movies, lectures, and classes. The staff of Wyoming's Heart Mountain camp included forty-two instructors. Each week they led twenty-seven activities in which six thousand internees participated. These included courses in calligraphy, bonsai gardening, and haiku, a traditional Japanese form of poetry. Issei mother Tei Tomita spent her days at Heart Mountain attending poetry classes. She soon after began keeping a journal in which she wrote her thoughts and poems. One 1943 poem reflects the comfort Tomita derived from writing: "Within the iron stockade/Always composing poems/From the sorrows of war/A little consolation."[46]

While lessons in haiku and bonsai provided some relief from the monotony, camp policy dictated that other, more American pastimes be encouraged as well. This included instruction in wood carving as well as sewing and knitting. Yet for many families, month upon month of internment took a toll. Gradually, mothers and fathers relinquished control over their children, knowing that their offspring could not venture far. "I think parental control became fairly lax," remembers former internee San Ono, "because where could you go? They knew that you were in the confines of the camp, and if you were in Block 35, the farthest you could be is Block 12. So parents didn't really worry about where their children were. I think that, to me, was one of the tragedies of being interned."[47]

Nisei, meanwhile, wandered the camps bored, frustrated, and resentful. Gradually, families became disconnected and alienated from one another. Close-knit families unraveled, worn down and exhausted by their open-ended detainment. "My own family, after three years of mess hall living, collapsed as an integrated unit," says Jeanne Wakatsuki Houston. "Whatever dignity or filial strength we may have known before December 1941 was lost."[48]

Resistance

At times these feelings of loss and hopelessness led to rebellion. Resistance to internment was not widespread or frequent, but it did exist.

At Poston, Heart Mountain, Topaz, and Tule Lake, angry internees complained about differences in pay and the availability of sugar. Conflicts also arose between younger and older camp residents. Rumors also spread about the existence of camp informers, Japanese who spied on their fellow internees for the FBI.

Young internees attend classes while living at the Minidoka relocation center in Idaho. Residents who had previously worked as teachers and doctors or who held jobs in other professions and trades put their skills to work in the camps.

The most violent uprising occurred at Manzanar. There, animosity developed between supporters of the JACL and Kibei, young people who had been educated in Japan. Shortages of sugar and meat led some in the camp to believe that camp administrators were earning money by selling the dietary staples on the camp's black market, thus depriving the general population. Tensions came to a boil when a JACL leader named Fred Tayama was attacked by six men wearing masks.

After an internal investigation camp authorities arrested the leader of the Kitchen Workers Union, Harry Ueno. In an attempt to defuse the situation, the camp director removed Ueno from Manzanar, but the action backfired when three thousand to four thousand internees marched to the administration area and protested Ueno's banishment. Under intense pressure, camp administrators relented and brought Ueno back to the camp, which displeased JACL supporters. Hundreds lashed out, and military police responded with tear gas.

In the growing chaos, a group of protesters pushed a truck toward the camp jail. Police fired their rifles. When the smoke cleared, a seventeen-year-old Japanese American was dead. Another victim, only twenty-one years old, died a few days later from a gunshot to the stomach. "That night was terrifying," says John Y. Tateishi, whose father was wrongly implicated in the riot plot. "All night long, the searchlights swept the camp, and bands of men could be heard running past our barracks, shouting angrily. We had no idea what had happened to my father."[49]

This sense of fear and alienation affected thousands of people in the camps. As a young man, Pat Morita was sent with his family to the Gila River internment camp in Arizona. Morita later became famous as an actor, best remembered for the 1984 movie *The Karate Kid*. He recalls his camp experience with bitterness and irony. "I remember doing the Pledge of Allegiance at the beginning of the school day," says Morita. "It was in a barracks. (I remember) my English class; and looking out the window and seeing the American flag waving, juxtaposed against a guard tower in the background, I had this sense of 'What's this all about?' Why am I saying 'liberty and justice for all?'"[50]

Loyalty and Renunciation

This conflicted sense of loyalty to the United States put internees in a psychologically fragile position. So, too, did a government-imposed loyalty oath that all camp residents seventeen years or older were required to sign beginning in February 1943. The oath was, in fact, a test created by the US Army and the WRA. Most of its questions were inoffensive and simple and asked for prior addresses and educational information. But two questions stirred anger among many internees. Question number twenty-seven asked, "Are you willing to serve in the armed forces of the United States on combat duty wherever ordered?" Question number twenty-eight asked, "Will you swear unqualified allegiance to the United States of America and faithfully defend the United States from any or all attack by foreign or domestic forces and forswear any form of allegiance or obedience to the Japanese emperor, to any other foreign government, power, or organization?"[51]

The irony could not have been lost on the internees, all of whom had until recently been considered threats to the United States. For Issei, unwelcome for so long, letting go of their allegiance to Japan presented a complicated conundrum: With no claim to American citizenship, giving up their Japanese citizenship meant abandoning claim to the only country that accepted them. Their Nisei children, meanwhile, still chafed at their treatment by the country of their birth. Since January 1942 they had been barred from serving in the military; now their government wanted them back.

Answering these pointed questions proved heart-wrenching for many and committed them to separate fates. A "no" answer to either question resulted in a transfer to the camp at Tule Lake. Those Nisei men responding in the affirmative became soldiers in the 442nd Regimental Combat Team, which later became part of the Hawaiian Nisei 100th Infantry Battalion. Women often took on roles as nurses or administrators. Still, many Nisei remained deeply resentful of what they considered a hypocritical turnaround. "They rob us of our property," says one unnamed Nisei man, "throw us into concentration camps, knock us down, spit on us and then invite us to 'prove' our loyalty by volunteering to go into an all-Nisei suicidal combat team to be thrown into front-line fighting."[52]

Whether they remained in the internment camps or went off to fight in Europe or the Pacific, the lives of these Japanese Americans were about to change. Although their imprisonment was soon to end, their fight for honor, respect, and justice had only just begun. It would last for more than four decades.

Chapter 4

Rulings, Release, and Repatriation

Born in 1924, African American novelist and social critic James Baldwin felt the sting of prejudice and racism all of his life. Baldwin was a contemporary of the Nisei who, along with their parents and grandparents, were imprisoned in internment camps throughout the United States. Baldwin believed that listening to the stories of those oppressed in a society provided a sense of a nation's standards of justice. "If one really wishes to know how justice is administered in a country," he writes, "one does not question the policemen, the lawyers, the judges, or the protected members of the middle class. One goes to the unprotected—those, precisely, who need the law's protection most!—and listens to their testimony."[53] By 1944 the voices of Japanese Americans remained mostly muted. Yet glimmers of hope for release and repatriation as equal citizens began to appear.

The Politics of Internment

Three years into the war, American attitudes about people of Japanese heritage remained bigoted. A majority of Americans still believed that Japanese Americans and their families had spied on their nation for the government in Japan. Nonetheless, clearer heads were beginning to prevail as a number of widely read magazines—including the *Nation* and *New Republic*—began publishing stories that showed Japanese Americans in a positive light. Hollywood did its part as well, as popular celebrities including comedian Bob Hope and singer Frank Sinatra spoke glowingly about the Japanese American soldiers they had met during their travels with the USO, an organization devoted to providing live entertainment to servicemen and servicewomen around the world.

Dillon S. Myer, too, appeared to be changing his mind about the internees under his control. After much consideration, Myer had come to believe that Japanese Americans no longer posed a threat to the West Coast of the United States. In March 1943 he wrote a letter to Henry L. Stimson that reflects this stunning turnaround and a clear recognition that the government's policies were discriminatory. "After many months of operating relocation centers," Myer writes, "the War Relocation Authority is convinced that they are undesirable institutions and should be removed from the American scene as soon as possible. . . . [Internment] has added weight to the contention of the enemy that . . . this nation preaches democracy and practices racial discrimination."[54] Myer's strong words were rejected out of hand by Stimson, who believed that the danger posed by the internees remained real.

Like Myer, Secretary of the Interior Harold Ickes doubted both the effectiveness and the justice of keeping more than one hundred thousand innocent people locked up. In a letter to President Roosevelt dated April 13, 1943, Ickes shares what he knew about the conditions of the internment camps and his belief that forced imprisonment could, in the end, turn Japanese Americans against their own country: "Information that has come to me from several sources is to the effect that the situation in at least some of the Japanese internment camps is bad and is becoming worse rapidly," he writes. "The result has been the gradual turning of thousands of well-meaning and loyal Japanese into angry prisoners. . . . [This] bodes no good for the future."[55]

Internment lost one of its staunchest defenders when Lieutenant General John L. DeWitt was replaced as chief of the army's Western Defense Command at the end of 1943. In February 1944, Myer's WRA was placed under the jurisdiction of Ickes's Department of the Interior. Believing that he now had the authority to directly comment on Japanese internment, Ickes shared his deep concerns about the program with Roosevelt. He then asked the president to repeal the exclusion orders that led to the internment. Roosevelt refused.

As the war went on, some US officials and influential magazines began questioning the government's internment actions. But many average citizens still saw their Japanese American neighbors as the enemy, as illustrated by this photograph taken in Washington in March 1944.

The Roosevelt administration no longer seriously feared a fifth column attack, and the war abroad appeared to be gradually winding down. But with the 1944 presidential election quickly approaching, the president wanted to protect himself—and his electoral chances—from any negative publicity. American internment policy would officially remain in place, but as more young internees left the camps under WRA leave programs, the practice would, Roosevelt believed, eventually come to an end. That June he said as much: "The more I think of this problem of suddenly ending the orders excluding Japanese Americans from the West Coast, the more I think it would be a mistake to do anything drastic or sudden. . . . I think the whole problem, for the sake of internal quiet, should be handled gradually."[56]

Court Challenges

While government officials continued debating the legality and validity of internment, several court cases promised to confront head on the relocation and detention of Japanese Americans. One of the first was the case of a young lawyer named Minoru Yasui. Trained as an American army officer and a prominent leader in the JACL, Yasui railed against the original exclusion orders and protested curfew orders known as Public Proclamation No. 3. The proclamation stated that Japanese Americans had to remain indoors from 8:00 p.m. to 6:00 a.m.

On the day the proclamation went into effect—March 28, 1942—Yasui flagrantly disregarded it. He stayed out past 8:00 p.m., wandering the streets near his home in Portland, Oregon, hoping he would be stopped and arrested. At 11:00 p.m. he walked to a nearby police station and pleaded with the officers until they arrested him. Yasui strongly believed that the imposed curfew violated the US Constitution because, he later said, "it makes distinctions between citizens on the basis of ancestry."[57]

While awaiting trial Yasui was told to report to a nearby assembly center. When he refused the order, police escorted him there. After weeks of temporary detention he was transferred to Minidoka Relocation Center in Idaho. When Yasui's case went before the US district court in Oregon, the presiding judge, James Alger Fee, agreed that the curfew proclamation was unconstitutional in relation to American citizens. But, Fee noted, Yasui had renounced his US citizenship by previously doing legal work for the Japanese consulate. The judge sentenced Yasui to one year in prison and a $5,000 fine. Nonetheless, Yasui's case set an important precedent: Those who protested the government's internment of Japanese Americans would have their day in court.

Another who protested the government's policies regarding Japanese Americans was Gordon Hirabayashi. Hirabayashi's parents were pacifists, meaning they did not believe in fighting. Hirabayashi followed their lead as a student at the University of Washington, but when the West Coast curfew was imposed, he ignored it. He also refused to register at a local processing center and was arrested. From May to Oc-

President Franklin D. Roosevelt (left) speaks at Fenway Park in Boston two days before the November 1944 presidential election. Wanting to avoid publicity that might hurt his chances for reelection, Roosevelt rejected calls to repeal the exclusion orders that led to the internment program.

tober 1942 Hirabayashi sat in a jail cell waiting for his court date to arrive. When it did, a federal jury in Seattle found him guilty of violating curfew laws and internment orders. More jail time followed.

Rulings

In May 1943 Hirabayashi and Yasui's appeals were presented in front of the US Supreme Court. Because the circumstances of the cases were similar, the justices considered the two at the same time. On June 21 the court handed down its ruling: Hirabayashi and Yasui were guilty

Censoring the Mail

In the years before texting, social media, and e-mail, people often wrote letters to one another as a way of keeping in touch. For Japanese Americans trapped behind fences and watched by armed guards, such correspondence provided a vital, even lifesaving connection to friends and family far away. The Prisoner of War unit run by the US government had the task of sorting through the masses of mail from the internment camps to look for suspicious letters or dangerous packages.

Located in Chicago, the unit employed more than one hundred workers who sat at long tables digging through piles of paper. On average, each censor went through fifty letters per day, looking for anything they deemed remotely unacceptable. With little consistency, censors might flag a letter writer's note about the cold weather, a humorous greeting to a friend, or an innocent photograph. The close and time-consuming scrutiny of camp correspondence could delay letters for weeks or even months. And Japanese Americans were not the only people subjected to mail censorship. During World War II, fourteen thousand workers opened 1 million pieces of mail per day in the United States in the hope of finding any tidbit of information that could help the war effort. In time, Americans became used to seeing a sticker with the words "Opened by Censor" on it.

of flouting curfew laws and disobeying evacuation orders. The court's reasoning hinged on national security, according to Associate Justice Hugo Black: "The immediate responsibility for defense must necessarily rest on those who direct our armed forces,"[58] he wrote in the majority opinion.

Another associate justice, Frank Murphy, felt less certain about the ruling than Black. Although he joined the side against the Japanese American plaintiffs, he believed that racism remained a core component of the case. Furthermore, Murphy suggested that the issue bore a stark resemblance to Nazi treatment of Jews before and during World War II. "Today is the first time, so far as I am aware, that we have sustained a substantial restriction of the personal liberty of citizens of the United States based upon the accident of race or ancestry," wrote Murphy in a draft dissent. "In this sense it bears a melancholy resemblance to the treatment accorded to members of the Jewish race in Germany and other parts of Europe."[59]

These two dramatic challenges to the US government's curfew and internment policies were soon followed by two more high-profile cases. One was the case of Nisei Fred Korematsu. In 1942 Korematsu went so far as to have plastic surgery on his eyes to make him look white as a way to avoid being sent to an internment camp. He also changed his name to Clyde Sarah, telling authorities that he was of Hawaiian and Spanish heritage. They did not believe him and instead arrested him on May 30, 1942. He was convicted that September, given probation, and sent to live first in the Tanforan assembly center and later the Topaz internment camp. When his case reached the US Supreme Court it, too, ruled against Korematsu on the grounds that Japanese Americans were often disloyal.

The only case decided in favor of a Japanese American plaintiff, and the one that had the most dramatic immediate impact on internment, was that of Mitsuye Endo. Incarcerated at the Tule Lake camp, Endo had no connection to the government in Japan, and her brother was an American soldier. For these reasons, civil rights lawyer James Purcell believed her case could help break the Roosevelt administration's policy of internment. With Purcell's help, Endo, a clerk by profession, became the only female resister. In 1942 Purcell filed a petition of habeas corpus, which insists that a person must be released from detention unless there is evidence to prove that he or she may have committed a crime.

The courts rejected the petition, and Endo was relocated to Topaz. Her case was argued before the Supreme Court in October 1944;

the ruling was handed down on December 18, the same day on which the *Korematsu* ruling was announced. But while the nine justices ruled against *Korematsu*, they ruled unanimously in favor of Endo, finding her utterly loyal to the United States and admitting the part that racism played in the internment policy: "Detention in Relocation Centers of persons of Japanese ancestry . . . is an example of the unconstitutional resort to racism inherent in the entire evacuation program."[60] Historians continue to debate why such similar cases were decided in opposing ways. The *Korematsu* case dealt specifically with exclusion and not detention, although in reality one consequently led to the other. The government could, according to the *Korematsu* decision, punish someone for refusing to be illegally detained; the *Endo* case held that this kind of detention is illegal.

End of Exclusion Order

Many observers wondered at the timing of the *Endo* decision. Only the day before—December 17, 1944—Roosevelt had signed Public Proclamation No. 21, which announced an end to the exclusion order that had kept so many Japanese Americans from their West Coast homes. Might the Supreme Court's *Endo* decision have been withheld one day to produce the appearance that the president and not the courts had effectively ended the internment policy? What is clear is that although the exclusion order was canceled, the government admitted no wrongdoing and made no apologies for the three-year imprisonment of more than one hundred thousand of its citizens.

The Jerome, Arkansas, camp closed on June 30, 1944, but the others remained open, at least for a while. On April 12, 1945, Roosevelt died from a stroke. Less than a month later, on May 8, the official end to the war in Europe came when Nazi Germany surrendered unconditionally to the Allied forces. But the war in the Pacific raged on, as the Empire of Japan refused to give in and the Allies launched a fierce and deadly firebombing campaign on the Asian nation, killing between 250,000 and 900,000 civilians. In late July delegations from the United States, the United Kingdom, and the Republic of China attended the Potsdam

Tōyō Miyatake: Documenting Injustice

Born in Tokyo, Japan, in 1896, Tōyō Miyatake came to the United States at the age of fourteen. He settled with his father in the Little Tokyo section of Los Angeles and developed an interest in photography. In 1923 Miyatake opened his own studio and befriended a promising young photographer named Edward Weston. Meanwhile, Miyatake continued taking pictures, mostly of people and places in his neighborhood.

By the beginning of World War II, Miyatake's reputation as a talented artist preceded him, yet it did not save him and his family from being relocated to California's Manzanar internment camp. Cameras were not allowed there; the government did not want its internees to document their experience. Still, Miyatake was determined to record the truth of the camps. Before his forced removal he had hidden a camera lens and a roll or two of film in his luggage. After arriving at Manzanar he found scraps of wood and built a working camera. Thereafter, he spent his days photographing life in the camp.

Later, Miyatake's old friend Weston, now a famous photographer, helped convince the camp director to allow Miyatake to use his own equipment. After the war ended and Miyatake returned home, he reopened his studio and moved on with his life. He died in 1979. Today visitors to Little Tokyo will see a statue of Tōyō Miyatake and can walk a street that bears his name.

Conference in defeated Germany. Subsequently, the participants issued the Potsdam Declaration, which called for Japan to surrender or face "prompt and utter destruction."[61] Still, the crippled country's military leaders refused to stand down.

While at Potsdam, new US president Harry S. Truman ordered the long-in-development atomic bomb to be dropped on a Japanese city if Japan did not surrender by August 3. The date passed with no word from Japan, and on August 6, 1945, an American B-29 bomber, the *Enola Gay*, dropped the world's first nuclear bomb, nicknamed "Little Boy," on the Japanese city of Hiroshima. The fireball and mushroom cloud created by the powerful device incinerated buildings, people, and anything else in its path. Three days later American airmen dropped a second atomic bomb, this time on the Japanese city of Nagasaki. On August 14 a devastated Japan officially surrendered. World War II was at an end, yet the fates of so many Japanese Americans were left unresolved.

Going Home

In October 1945 camps closed in Granada, Colorado; Minidoka, Idaho; and Topaz, Utah. A month later others began shutting down in Gila River, Arizona; Heart Mountain, Wyoming; Manzanar, California; Poston, Arizona; and Rohwer, Arkansas. The internees were free to leave, but at first thousands chose to stay. Three years of around-the-clock surveillance, shabby accommodations, and food shortages had become a habit—a way of life—for thousands, and what exactly their future held remained unknown. "The news of being able to go back to California has been accepted with mingled feelings," wrote Fusa Tsumagari from Poston camp in Arizona. "Those with property are wanting to go back, but wondering how the sentiment will be. Of course we know that good friends . . . would be glad to have us back but others who do not know us or understand us may not be as glad to see us."[62]

This sense of ambivalence on the part of those now free left many wondering what exactly they had to return to. Their property and possessions had been sold long ago; they had no jobs and little money. "Getting back," says former internee Aya Nakamura, "I was shocked to see what had happened, our home being bought by a different family, different decorations in the windows; it was our house, but it wasn't anymore."[63]

A massive mushroom-shaped cloud forms over Nagasaki, Japan, after US forces dropped an atomic bomb on the city on August 9, 1945. The US bombing of Hiroshima and Nagasaki effectively ended the war with Japan.

Many feared that they might again become victims of racism and prejudice. The WRA authorities had no choice but to let those in need of food and shelter stay on at the camps until they found somewhere to go. When these former prisoners did leave, each was given twenty-five dollars and a one-way train ticket home to California, Oregon, Washington, or wherever they came from.

Tule Lake, the last of the camps to close, did not shutter its doors until March 1946. By then thousands of Japanese American families had already found some semblance of a new life. Fathers and mothers took any jobs they could find, and they lived wherever they could find room, whether it be church social halls, rooms in private houses, or modest trailer camps. Jeanne Wakatsuki Houston's family received help from the American Friends Service Committee, one of dozens of charity groups that worked to get former internees reintegrated into American life. The Wakatsukis soon moved into a housing project apartment in west Long Beach, California. "At the time it seemed to be a big step up in the world," says Houston. "There would be no more standing in chow lines; now mama had a stove to cook on. We had three bedrooms. And we had an inside toilet. . . . Papa went in and flushed it, and when it worked, we all hooted with delight."[64]

"What You Have Done for This Country"

As Japanese American families began piecing their lives back together, Truman paused to honor a group of unlikely heroes. On July 15, 1946, Truman spoke to the 100th Battalion and 442nd Regimental Combat Team made up of young Japanese Americans, most whom had spent some time in internment camps. In his remarks, Truman reflected on the soldiers' battle not only against American enemies but also American intolerance. The speech reflected the stunning turnaround of a government that until recently had eyed these soldiers and their families with suspicion. "I can't tell you how much I appreciate the opportunity to tell you what you have done for this country," said Truman. "You fought not only the enemy, but you fought prejudice. And you won. You have made the Constitution stand for what it really means: the welfare of all the people, all the time."[65]

Two years later Congress passed the Evacuation Claims Act of 1948, which compensated Japanese Americans for property lost or damaged during their internment. But former internees were provided with financial compensation of less than 10 percent of what their lost or sold properties were worth. The pain and suffering of those imprisoned for more than three years was largely ignored. In addition, officials failed to acknowledge an injustice that tore at the very fabric of a nation built on the rule of law. For the next two decades the issue of Japanese American internment languished. Those seeking to right the wrong were told to stay silent: The war was over and it was time to move on. Yet for many the painful memories lingered, as did persistent feelings of betrayal and abandonment.

Chapter 5

What Is the Legacy of the Japanese Internment Camps?

Long after the last internees folded their clothes, packed their bags, and set off to pick up the scattered pieces of their broken lives, the internment of Japanese Americans hovered over the nation like an ominous shadow. The memory of that time haunted Americans from all walks of life and of all ethnic backgrounds. A government policy that began in hysteria and fear became, in time, a symbol of a nation's prejudice and misguided attempt at protecting itself from an internal threat that did not exist.

In the decades after the internment many Americans tried to forget and put the past behind them. But the Japanese American families—Issei and Nisei alike—could not forget. They fought for their voices to be heard and their grievances aired. Most wanted little more than an apology, a recognition that their pain was real, and that the country they loved—had fought for and, in many cases, died for—cared. They also hoped to pass on the legacy of their history, their belief that Americans, no matter where they came from or what they believed, deserved to be treated equally under the law.

Fighting for Recognition

Twenty years after the end of World War II, a former internee named Edison Uno broke his silence. Born in Los Angeles, California, in 1929,

Uno was sent with his family to the Granada relocation camp in Colorado in 1942. Soon after, he was transferred to the Crystal City camp in Texas. After the war Uno earned a degree in political science from Los Angeles State College. His internment experience inspired him to become involved in civil rights, and in the early 1970s he and a small group of Japanese Americans began speaking about what had happened to them. By talking publicly about their experiences, they felt they could help prevent such hysteria and racism from happening to immigrants and their families in the future.

Not all members of the Japanese American community were as enthusiastic as Uno and his group. For them, forgetting the past and never discussing it seemed the best way to move on with their lives. The pain and hardship suffered in those years had led to shame for some of them; others even blamed themselves for their incarceration. Worst of all, many believed, reviving the issue could lead to renewed prejudice against all things Japanese. Yet Uno remained determined to bring the internment camps into the public spotlight. "It seems to me," he says, "that we who have survived the experience have a responsibility to make certain our perspectives are documented in the many interpretations of this historic event in our lives."[66]

Uno's passion for the issue of internment led him to begin researching and documenting the anti-Asian and anti-Japanese fervor present in American life in the years before Pearl Harbor. He published articles chronicling the racist views of American politicians and public officials, the laws that cracked down on Japanese Americans, and the denial of basic rights guaranteed by the US Constitution. Uno's work slowly shook loose old memories and gave many Nisei like himself the confidence to speak out.

The Movement Grows

In the mid-1970s, the efforts of Uno and others became known as the redress movement. It was inspired in part by the civil rights movement of the 1950s and 1960s, during which African Americans fought for equal rights. While some Nisei were involved in the movement, many of them believed it better to simply try to forget. A third generation of Japanese Americans, known as *Sansei*, disagreed and provided the major impetus behind the redress movement.

On college campuses across the nation, Sansei researched the history of the Nisei and Issei and tried to educate their fellow students about the internment. At the same time, the Japanese American Citizens League became involved. At the JACL national convention in 1976, the league adopted a resolution calling for financial reparations, or compensation, for all those who suffered during the war. Specifically, the JACL called for $25,000 for each person imprisoned, an apology from Congress, and the creation of an educational foundation for the children of formerly interned Japanese Americans.

To this end, redress advocates lobbied their representatives in Congress and other officials in the government, asking them to acknowledge the wrong that had been done to their families. These efforts paid off that same year when Gerald R. Ford became the first American president to directly address the internment, calling it a "national mistake" and promising "that this kind of action shall never again be repeated."[67]

Federal Recognition

Ford's statement brought the issue into the public discourse and prompted more Americans than ever before to consider the tragedy of internment. In 1980 Congress established the Commission on Wartime Relocation and Internment of Civilians (CWRIC) to thoroughly research the matter. In 1983, after three years of work, the commission published *Personal Justice Denied*. The report criticized Executive Order 9066 and determined that prejudice and war hysteria rather than national security led to the denial of basic rights to Japanese Americans and their families, stating, "Widespread ignorance of Japanese Americans contributed to a policy conceived in haste and executed in an atmosphere of fear and anger at Japan. A grave injustice was done."[68] The report subsequently called for a congressional apology to the victims and a payment of $20,000 to each surviving internee.

In 1980 President Jimmy Carter signs the act that created the Commission on Wartime Relocation and Internment of Civilians. In its 1983 report the commission criticized the internment program as the product of prejudice and war hysteria rather than any actual threats to national security.

It took five more years of legal wrangling for Japanese Americans to receive some measure of justice, but on August 10, 1988, President Ronald Reagan signed the Civil Liberties Act into law. In his remarks, Reagan refused to cast blame yet conceded that a grievous wrong had been committed: "Yes, the nation was then at war, struggling for its survival—and it's not for us to pass judgment upon those who may have made mistakes while engaged in that great struggle. Yet we must recognize that the internment of Japanese Americans was just that—a mistake. For throughout the war, Japanese Americans in the tens of thousands remained utterly loyal to the United States."[69]

The law created a ten-year program with the intent of compensating those Japanese Americans interned during World War II. It included an acknowledgement of wrongdoing and an apology. Those applying for

What's in a Name?

For people whose lives were forever altered by internment, the words chosen to describe those years can make all the difference in how history is written. At the time, the US government referred to the Japanese American camps as "War Relocation Centers." Yet the word "internment," meaning confinement, seems a more precise description. Those who lived in the camps were not only relocated far from their homes but forced to live there.

In recent years some commentators and historians have used the term *concentration camps* to describe the facilities in which people of Japanese heritage were placed. Others chafe at those words because they are forever linked to the systematic slaughter of Jews, Slavs, and other ethnic groups by the Nazis in the 1930s and 1940s. According to historian Joseph R. Conlin, the internment camps cannot be equated with Nazi concentration camps. "Life in the camps was humiliating," says Conlin, "but there was not cruelty, brutality, or forced labor, let alone murder." The Nazi camps, though, are more accurately labeled "death camps," factories built specifically to kill thousands, even millions, of people. Historian Roger Daniels argues that the term *internment camps* should be dropped in favor of *concentration camps* when talking about the Japanese American experience. He prefers the definition given at the US Holocaust Memorial Museum: "The term *concentration camp* refers to a camp in which people are detained or confined, usually under harsh conditions and without regard to legal norms of arrest and imprisonment that are acceptable in a constitutional democracy."

Joseph R. Conlin, *The American Past: A Survey of American History: Since 1865*. Independence, KY: Cengage, 2009, p. 708.

Quoted in Edward Schumacher-Matos and Lori Grisham, "Euphemisms, Concentration Camps, and the Japanese Internment," National Public Radio, February 10, 2012. www.npr.org.

compensation had to be of Japanese ancestry or be closely related to such a person. Also, they had to be a US citizen or a permanent resident alien, a label given to most Issei at the time of internment. Finally, only those evacuated, relocated, or interned could apply.

The first government payments of $20,000 were sent on October 9, 1990. For the next decade, until February 5, 1999, the Office of Redress Administration remained open. By the time it closed, 82,250 people had claimed a total of $1.6 billion.

Legal Legacy

The same year that the CWRIC published its report condemning internment and calling for redress, historian Peter Irons made a discovery that would transform the legal legacy of those harrowing years. While digging through government archives, Irons came upon World War II–era documents from a variety of federal agencies that clearly proved Japanese Americans had posed no security or military threat to the United States. Furthermore, the documents had been intentionally hidden from Supreme Court justices during their review of Fred Korematsu's trial in 1944.

For forty years, Korematsu had lived with the dishonor of having been convicted of disloyalty to his country. Through it all he had remained a loyal American, but in legal terms his conviction stood. Irons's research forced the federal courts to reopen Korematsu's case on the basis of government misconduct, and on November 10, 1983, a federal court judge in San Francisco overturned Korematsu's decades-old conviction. Those in attendance, many of them former camp prisoners themselves, cheered the decision.

In 1984 Minoru Yasui's case was reopened in a federal district court. As in the *Korematsu* case, Yasui's conviction was overturned, yet the court refused to comment on Yasui's claims of misconduct on the part of the prosecution. Yasui died in 1986. Gordon Hirabayashi's infamous wartime trial was reexamined by a federal district court in 1987. Like the others, the sixty-nine-year-old Hirabayashi sought exoneration for any wrongdoing. He received it when the court vacated his conviction.

"There was a time when I felt that the Constitution failed me," he said afterward. "But with the reversal in the courts and in public statements from the government, I feel that our country has proven that the Constitution is worth upholding. The U.S. government admitted it made a mistake. A country that can do that is a strong country. I have more faith and allegiance to the Constitution than I ever had before."[70]

Satsuki Ina, who was born in the Tule Lake internment camp in California, displays the check and letter of apology she received from President Bill Clinton in 2001. Congress authorized a ten-year program to compensate former internees and their families.

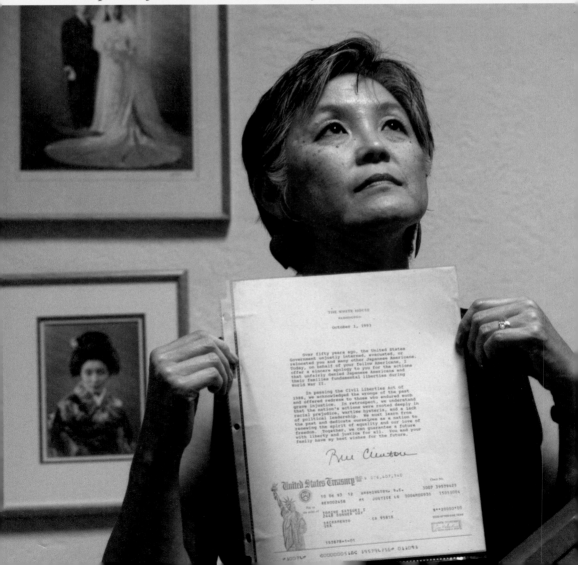

The *Hirabayashi* case, the last of its kind, represented the final legal obstacle to righting a past wrong that had long haunted the nation. When the conviction fell apart, the lasting legacy of Japanese American internment came into view. "What is particularly noteworthy about the confinement of the Issei and Nisei is its fundamentally ironic character," says historian Greg Robinson. "It was an arbitrary and antidemocratic measure put into effect by a government devoted to humanitarian aims, which occurred as a part of a war the nation was waging for the survival of world freedom."[71]

Twenty-First Century Fears

Echoes of Japanese American internment surfaced in the wake of the terrorist attacks of September 11, 2001, which killed nearly three thousand Americans, and the enduring strength of the United States was severely tested. The nineteen terrorists who carried out the attacks were followers of Islam. Consequently, some American legislators and commentators suggested segregating all Muslim Americans in camps similar to those used for Japanese Americans during World War II. This way, they argued, Muslim extremists could be more closely monitored and prevented from perpetrating other acts of terror or collaborating with terrorists.

To many in the Muslim American population, the scrutiny and condemnation they received in the weeks and months after 9/11 already made them feel like prisoners in their own country, although they had done nothing wrong. "The Muslim community in the United States has been living in a virtual internment camp ever since 9/11," says Abdul Malik Mujahid of the Muslim Peace Coalition. "Since then, more than 700,000 Muslims have been interviewed by the FBI. . . . Practically all mosques have been 'checked for nuclear bombs' or other fear-provoking reasons. That's the level of trust we 'enjoy' in the Muslim community."[72]

Most Americans quickly rejected the idea of constructing internment camps for Muslims. In a 2004 newspaper article, civil rights pioneer Fred Korematsu spoke out against any such notion. He reminded Americans that a rush to judgment can have fateful consequences:

> I know what it is like to be at the other end of such scapegoating and how difficult it is to clear one's name after unjustified suspicions are endorsed as fact by the government. If someone is a spy or terrorist they should be prosecuted for their actions.

A San Francisco Bay Area teacher whose uncle fought the order to report to an internment camp talks to her students about his efforts on Fred Korematsu Day. Korematsu's story continues to inspire young people.

But no one should ever be locked away simply because they share the same race, ethnicity, or religion as a spy or terrorist. If that principle was not learned from the internment of Japanese Americans, then these are very dangerous times for our democracy.[73]

Korematsu died less than a year later, on March 30, 2005, at the age of eighty-six. After his release from camp, he had married and started a family. Yet his conviction on charges of disloyalty to the United States haunted him. He feared that his children would be stigmatized because of their Japanese ancestry just as he had been. He kept his youthful protest and Supreme Court case to himself. Only in performing research for a high school book report did his daughter learn about her father's past.

In the years since Korematsu's death, his home state of California has honored his legacy of fighting for civil rights by naming three schools after him. In the fall of 2010, the California legislature passed the Fred Korematsu Day of Civil Liberties and the Constitution bill, which designated January 30 of each year as a day to honor him. It was the first day in US history dedicated to honoring an Asian American. Korematsu's story continues to inspire young people. In an economically deprived neighborhood of East Oakland, the mostly black and Hispanic students begin every Monday morning with a special cheer that honors both the legacy of Korematsu and the 120,000 Japanese Americans interned in relocation camps: "Korematsu! We stand up for what is right!"[74]

Lasting Legacy

Perhaps the greatest legacy of the Japanese American internment camps is the resilience of the people that lived through it. They returned to the general population, remade their lives and thrived, despite a history of hardship and discrimination. While many remain uncomfortable talking about their wartime experiences in places like Topaz, Manzanar,

Landmarks of Memory

One of the lasting legacies of the Japanese American internment experience is the memories enshrined in the camps themselves. To help preserve those memories for future generations, the California State Department of Parks and Recreation designated Manzanar as a State Historical Landmark in 1972. In February 1985 Manzanar was designated as a National Historic Landmark. In the early 1990s President George H.W. Bush, a World War II veteran, placed Manzanar under the control and stewardship of the National Park Service.

Today, ten of the former camps are designated as historic landmarks. Each year hundreds of thousands of people from all over the world visit them. The tourists stroll the grounds, sit in reconstructions of internment camp barracks, and learn about the experience of Japanese Americans through interactive museum exhibits.

These remnants of history provide an up-close look at the challenges that Japanese Americans faced during their internment. For survivors of those camps, these national landmarks teach a valuable lesson that books alone cannot convey. "No one could really learn from the books," said former Manzanar resident Sue Kunitomi Embrey. "You have to walk through the blocks, see the gardens, and the remains of the stone walls and rocks." By doing so, visitors can reflect on the nation's past and remember those whose lives were forever altered by internment.

Quoted in National Park Service, "Manzanar: National Historic Site." www.nps.gov.

and Gila River, their children, grandchildren, and great-grandchildren are not so reluctant to speak out.

By doing so they lay claim to their heritage as Japanese Americans and keep alive the memories of those years for future generations. "Our experience was unique, but it's an example of the broader experience of racism, how it permeates lives, and how we each attempt to survive it," says family therapist and filmmaker Satsuki Ina. "It's about trauma and suffering, but it also is about our strength."[75]

Source Notes

Introduction: The Defining Characteristics of Japanese Internment

1. J. Hector St. John de Crèvecoeur, *Letters from an American Farmer*. Carlisle, MA: Applewood Books, 1904, p. 55.

Chapter One: What Conditions Led to Internment of Japanese Americans?

2. Guofang Li and Lihshing Wang, *Model Minority Myth Revisited: An Interdisciplinary Approach to Demystifying Asian American Educational Experience*. Charlotte, NC: Information Age, 2008, p. 38.

3. Quoted in Gary Noy, *Distant Horizon: Documents from the Nineteenth-Century American West*. Lincoln: University of Nebraska Press, 1999, p. 326.

4. Quoted in PBS Home Video, *Time of Fear*, 2004.

5. Quoted in Winston Press, *Red & Yellow, Black & Brown*. New York: Holt, Rinehart, and Winston, 1973, p. 129.

6. Quoted in Paul R. Spickard, *Japanese Americans: The Formation and Transformations of an Ethnic Group*. New Brunswick: Rutgers University Press, 2009, p. 63.

7. Quoted in Roger Daniels, *Guarding the Golden Door: American Immigration Policy and Immigrants Since 1882*. New York: Macmillan, 2004, pp. 42–43.

8. G.G. Rupert, *The Yellow Peril*. Britton, OK: Union, 1911, e-book.

9. Quoted in Brenda L. Moore, *Serving Our Country: Japanese American Women in the Military During World War II*. New Brunswick: Rutgers University Press, 2003, p. 37.

10. Quoted in Moore, *Serving Our Country*, p. 36.
11. Quoted in Legal Information Institute, "14th Amendment, U.S. Constitution," Cornell University Law School. www.law.cornell.edu.
12. Quoted in Paul R. Spickard, *Mixed Blood: Intermarriage and Ethnic Identity in Twentieth-Century America*. Madison: University of Wisconsin Press, 1991, p. 32.
13. Quoted in Spickard, *Mixed Blood*, p. 32.
14. Quoted in PBS Home Video, *Time of Fear*.
15. Quoted in Stephanie Bangarth, *Voices Raised in Protest: Defending North American Citizens of Japanese Ancestry, 1942–49*. Vancouver: University of British Columbia Press, 2008, p. 121.

Chapter Two: War and Evacuation

16. Quoted in Francis L. Loewenheim, Harold D. Langley, and Manfred Jonas, eds., *Roosevelt and Churchill: Their Secret Wartime Correspondence*. London: Barrie & Jenkins, 1975, p. 162.
17. Quoted in Howard Jones, *Crucible of Power: A History of U.S. Foreign Relations Since 1897*. Lanham, MD: Rowman & Littlefield, 2001, p. 182.
18. Quoted in Jones, *Crucible of Power*, p. 184.
19. Quoted in Joy Waldron Jasper, James P. Delgado, and Jim Adams, *The USS Arizona: The Ship, the Men, the Pearl Harbor Attack and the Symbol That Aroused America*. New York: St. Martin's, 2003, pp. 112–13.
20. Quoted in Greg Robinson, *A Tragedy of Democracy: Japanese Confinement in North America*. New York: Columbia University Press, 2009, p. 60.
21. Quoted in Paul Howard Takemoto, *Nisei Memories: My Parents Talk About the War Years*. Seattle: University of Washington Press, 2006, p. 27.
22. Quoted in PBS Home Video, *Time of Fear*.
23. Quoted in Francis MacDonnell, *Insidious Foes: The Axis Fifth Column and the American Home Front*. New York: Oxford University Press, 1995, p. 85.

24. Quoted in MacDonnell, *Insidious Foes*, p. 85.

25. Quoted in MacDonnell, *Insidious Foes*, p. 87.

26. Quoted in MacDonnell, *Insidious Foes*, p. 87.

27. Quoted in Joseph Tilden Rhea, *Race Pride and the American Identity*. Cambridge: Harvard University Press, 2001, p. 46.

28. Quoted in Rhea, *Race Pride and the American Identity*, p. 46.

29. Quoted in Rhea, *Race Pride and the American Identity*, pp. 45–46.

30. Quoted in PBS Home Video, *Time of Fear*.

31. Quoted in Richard Drinnon, *Keeper of Concentration Camps: Dillon S. Myer and American Racism*. Berkeley: University of California Press, 1987, p. 3.

32. Quoted in Ellen Eisenberg, "As Truly American as Your Son," *Oregon Historical Quarterly*, vol. 104, no. 4, 2003, p. 542.

33. Quoted in Robert K. Fitts, *The Japanese American Internment: Innocence, Guilt, and Wartime Justice*. Lincoln: University of Nebraska Press, 2008, p. 35.

Chapter Three: Life in Camps

34. Quoted in Loewenheim, Langley, and Jonas, *Roosevelt and Churchill*, pp. 291–92.

35. Quoted in Heather C. Lindquist, ed., *Children of Manzanar*. Berkeley: Heyday, 2012, p. 12.

36. Quoted in PBS Home Video, *Time of Fear*.

37. Quoted in Lindquist, *Children of Manzanar*, p. 6.

38. Quoted in Lindquist, *Children of Manzanar*, p. 20.

39. Quoted in PBS Home Video, *Time of Fear*.

40. Quoted in PBS Home Video, *Time of Fear*.

41. Quoted in PBS Home Video, *Time of Fear*.

42. Jeanne Wakatsuki Houston, *Farewell to Manzanar*. New York: Ember, 1973, p. 33.

43. Quoted in Samuel Walker, *Presidents and Civil Liberties from Wilson to Obama: A Story of Poor Custodians*. Cambridge: Cambridge University Press, 2012, p. 87.

44. Quoted in Deborah Gesenway, *Beyond Words: Images from America's Concentration Camps*. Ithaca: Cornell University Press, 1988, p. 126.

45. Quoted in Lindquist, *Children of Manzanar*, p. 23.

46. Quoted in Karen J. Blair, ed., *Women in Pacific Northwest History*, vol. 1. Seattle: University of Washington Press, 2001, p. 294.

47. Quoted in Lindquist, *Children of Manzanar*, p. 35.

48. Houston, *Farewell to Manzanar*, p. 37.

49. Quoted in Erica Harth, ed., *Last Witnesses: Reflections on the Wartime Internment of Japanese Americans*. New York: Palgrave Macmillan, 2003, p. 134.

50. Quoted in Charles C. Goodin, "Noriyuki Pat Morita: In the Footsteps of a Sensei," Seinenkai.com. http://seinenkai.com.

51. Quoted in Tetsuden Kashima, *Judgment Without Trial: Japanese American Imprisonment During World War II*. Seattle: University of Washington Press, 2003, p. 161.

52. Quoted in Kashima, *Judgment Without Trial*, p. 162.

Chapter Four: Rulings, Release, and Repatriation

53. James Baldwin, *The Price of the Ticket: Collected Nonfiction, 1948–1985*. New York: Macmillan, 1985, p. 527.

54. Quoted in Whitney Hartzel, *Introduction to U.S. Internment Camp History*, February 10, 2013. http://prezi.com.

55. Quoted in Deborah Gesenway and Mindy Roseman, *Beyond Words: Images from America's Concentration Camps*. Ithaca: Cornell University Press, 1988, p. 79.

56. Quoted in Commission on the Wartime Relocation and Internment of Civilians, *Personal Justice Denied*. Washington, DC: GPO, 1982, p. 229.

57. Quoted in Mitchell Takeshi Maki, Harry H.L. Kitano, and Sarah Megan Berthold, *Achieving the Impossible Dream: How Japanese Americans Obtained Redress*. Urbana: University of Illinois Press, 1999, p. 35.

58. Quoted in Roger K. Newman, *Hugo Black: A Biography*. New York: Fordham University Press, 1997, p. 314.

59. Quoted in James Sean Healey, *When I Was Not My Brother's Keeper: When Fear, Hate and Prejudice Administer the Law.* BookSurge, 2007, p. 85.

60. Quoted in Hyung-Chan Kim, ed., *Asian Americans and the Supreme Court: A Documentary History.* Santa Barbara: Greenwood, 1992, p. 52.

61. Quoted in E. Takemae, *The Allied Occupation of Japan.* New York: Continuum, 2003, p. 219.

62. Quoted in Smithsonian Education, "The Slow Return," *Letters from the Japanese American Internment.* 2012. www.smithsonian education.org.

63. Quoted in Grant Amann, "Executive Order 9066 Successes, Failures, and Consequences." http://27535443.nhd.weebly.com/then .html

64. Houston, *Farewell to Manzanar,* p. 138.

65. Quoted in National Park Service, "Manzanar: National Historic Site." www.nps.gov.

Chapter Five: What Is the Legacy of the Japanese Internment Camps?

66. Quoted in Clark Davis and David Igler, eds., *The Human Tradition in California.* Lanham, MD: Rowman & Littlefield, 2002, p. 162.

67. Quoted in Geoffrey R. Stone, *Perilous Times: Free Speech in Wartime from the Sedition Act of 1798 to the War on Terrorism.* New York: Norton, 2004, p. 305.

68. Quoted in Roger Daniels, Sandra C. Taylor, Harry H.L. Kitano, and Leonard J. Arrington, eds., *Japanese Americans: From Relocation to Redress.* Seattle: University of Washington Press, 2001, p. 5.

69. Quoted in Kermit L. Hall and John J. Patrick, *The Pursuit of Justice: Supreme Court Decisions That Shaped America.* New York: Oxford University Press, 2006, p. 110.

70. Quoted in Mark Memmott, "Gordon Hirabayashi Has Died; He Refused to Go to WWII Internment Camp," National Public Radio, January 4, 2012. www.npr.org.

71. Robinson, *A Tragedy of Democracy,* p. 1.

72. Quoted in Deepa Kumar, *Islamophobia and the Politics of Empire.* Chicago: Haymarket, 2012, p. 197.

73. Fred Korematsu, "Do We Really Need to Relearn the Lessons of Japanese American Internment?," *San Francisco Chronicle*, September 16, 2004. www.sfgate.com.

74. Quoted in Ling Woo Liu, "California Marks the First Fred Korematsu Day," *Time*, January 30, 2011. www.time.com.

75. Quoted in PBS, *Children of the Camps*, directed by Satsuki Ina, 2003. www.pbs.org.

Karl Bendetsen: The lawyer who, according to his own admission, conceived of and drafted Executive Order 9066, which provided the legal basis for the mass removal of 120,000 Japanese Americans during World War II. He later recanted, denying any responsibility for the evacuation decision.

Clara Breed: A children's book librarian in San Diego, California, who knew many of the Japanese American children interned in camps during World War II. She supplied the children with stamped postcards so they could communicate with her and mailed them candy, clothes, and books to help them through their ordeal.

Wayne Collins: An American attorney who worked to challenge evacuation orders and the internment of the Japanese by representing a number of clients, including Fred Korematsu and some of those Japanese Americans who renounced their citizenship.

John L. DeWitt: US Army general who recommended that people of Japanese heritage be evacuated from coastal regions and soon after, with the president's approval, ordered and organized their removal and relocation to internment camps.

William O. Douglas: Associate justice of the US Supreme Court who voted in 1944 to uphold the internment of Japanese Americans in *Korematsu v. United States*, but eventually became a leading voice for individual rights.

Mitsuye Endo: Japanese American secretary and typist who worked for California's Department of Motor Vehicles before being fired from her job and sent to an internment camp in Utah. She challenged her detainment and was deemed a loyal citizen in 1944.

William Randolph Hearst: Early twentieth-century newspaper magnate whose newspapers stoked anti-Japanese sentiment and promoted the concept of the "yellow peril."

Gordon Kiyoshi Hirabayashi: A Japanese American who, as a sociology student at the University of Washington, refused to be sent to an internment camp. Incarcerated at an Arizona work camp, he took his case to the Supreme Court in 1943.

Harold Ickes: US secretary of the interior during the Roosevelt administration and vocal critic of the internment of the Japanese and the conditions under which they were forced to live.

Fred Korematsu: A Japanese American and civil rights pioneer who refused to obey the American government's order to report to an internment camp. Arrested and jailed soon after, Korematsu took his case to the US Supreme Court, which ruled against him.

Dillon S. Myer: Head of the WRA, the government agency that oversaw the forced removal and resettlement of Japanese Americans from 1942 to 1946.

James Duval Phelan: Early twentieth-century mayor of San Francisco and later US senator noted for his anti-Japanese zeal. He supported alien land law legislation and the concept of the "yellow peril."

Ronald Reagan: Fortieth president of the United States, who signed the Civil Liberties Act of 1988, which granted financial reparations to formerly interned Japanese Americans.

Franklin Delano Roosevelt: Thirty-second president of the United States, who signed Executive Order 9066 on February 19, 1942. The order enabled American military powers to ban citizens from coastal regions in California and Washington State and to transport citizens to relocation centers.

Henry L. Stimson: Secretary of war during the Roosevelt administration who designated General John L. DeWitt as military commander with the authority to relocate Japanese Americans.

Earl Warren: Attorney general for the state of California during World War II and strong supporter of Japanese internment. After the Pearl Harbor attack, he helped organize California's civilian defense program as a way of guarding against a future Japanese onslaught. Later, during his tenure as Chief Justice of the Supreme Court, the court desegregated American schools in the decision *Brown v. Board of Education*.

Minoru Yasui: Japanese American attorney who worked to fight laws that discriminated against and targeted people of Japanese descent living in the United States. His case testing the constitutionality of enforced curfews went to the Supreme Court.

For Further Research

Books

Margaret Bane Eberle, *The Gem of the Desert: A Japanese-American Internment Camp*. Bloomington, IN: iUniverse, 2008.

Linda Gordon and Gary Y. Okihiro, eds., *Impounded: Dorothea Lange and the Censored Images of Japanese American Internment*. New York: Norton, 2008.

Kimi Cunningham Grant, *Silver Like Dust: One Family's Story of America's Japanese Internment*. New York: Pegasus, 2012.

Mary Matsuda Gruenewald, *Looking Like the Enemy: My Story of Imprisonment in Japanese American Internment Camps*. Troutdale, OR: NewSage, 2005.

Delphine Hirasuna, *The Art of Gaman: Arts and Crafts from the Japanese American Internment Camps, 1942–1946*. Emeryville, CA: Ten Speed, 2005.

Jeanne Houston and James D. Houston, *Farewell to Manzanar*. Fort Walton Beach, FL: Ember, 2012.

Angus Lorenzen, *A Lovely Little War: Life Through the Eyes of a Child Imprisoned in a Japanese Internment Camp*. Palisades, NY: History, 2008.

Websites

Children of the Camps (www.pbs.org/childofcamp/index.html). This companion website to the PBS series of the same name offers a detailed peek into the internment experience. The site includes an internment time line along with photographs and a fact sheet about the camps.

Conscience and the Constitution (www.resisters.com). Produced for PBS, this companion site for the documentary film of the same name provides an in-depth look at the Japanese American men who led an organized resistance to the World War II internment. The site's regular postings provide current information on Japanese Americans in the twenty-first century, along with links to relevant historical documents.

Japanese American National Museum (www.janm.org). Located in Los Angeles, this museum seeks to pay tribute to the experiences of Japanese Americans past and present. Perhaps most interesting and useful is the "Museum Collections" section, where researchers can find primary sources that include Clara Breed's letters, diaries of those interned during World War II, and thousands of photographs from the time.

National Park Service: Manzanar (www.nps.gov/manz/index.htm). Once an internment camp, Manzanar, located in California, now stands as a memorial to those once incarcerated there. The website is one of the best resources on the subject of internment camps and includes a photo gallery, a virtual tour of the camp, and many colorful online exhibits.

Virtual Museum of the City of San Francisco: Internment of San Francisco Japanese (www.sfmuseum.org/war/evactxt.html). This simple but valuable site provides links to news stories written about California's Japanese population at the time of internment. Readers can literally peer into the past for a better understanding of the prejudices and politics of the time.

Index

Note: Boldface page numbers indicate illustrations.

Picture Credits

Cover: © Hulton-Deutsch Collection/Corbis

Maury Aaseng: 43

Hector Amezcua/Zuma Press/Newscom: 74

AP Images: 47, 71

© Bettmann/Corbis: 19, 24, 33, 39, 51, 57, 59

© Paul Chinn/San Francisco Chronicle/Corbis: 76

© Corbis: 9, 65

Dorothea Lange, NC History Images/Newscom: 15

Thinkstock Images: 6, 7

About the Author

David Robson's many books include *Shakespeare's Globe Theater*, *Colonial America*, *Weapons and Defense Research*, and *The Decade of the 2000s*. He is also an award-winning playwright whose work for the stage has been performed across the country and abroad. Robson lives with his family in Wilmington, Delaware.